Clojure Reactive Programming

Design and implement highly reusable reactive applications by integrating different frameworks with Clojure

Leonardo Borges

[PACKT] open source *

PUBLISHING

community experience distilled

BIRMINGHAM - MUMBAI

Clojure Reactive Programming

First published: March 2015

Production reference: 1160315

Published by Packt Publishing Ltd.
Livery Place
35 Livery Street
Birmingham B3 2PB, UK.

ISBN 978-1-78398-666-8

www.packtpub.com

Credits

Author
Leonardo Borges

Reviewers
Eduard Bondarenko
Colin Jones
Michael Kohl
Falko Riemenschneider

Acquisition Editor
Harsha Bharwani

Content Development Editor
Arun Nadar

Technical Editor
Tanvi Bhatt

Copy Editors
Vikrant Phadke
Sameen Siddiqui

Project Coordinator
Neha Bhatnagar

Proofreaders
Simran Bhogal
Maria Gould

Indexer
Mariammal Chettiyar

Graphics
Abhinash Sahu

Production Coordinator
Manu Joseph

Cover Work
Manu Joseph

About the Author

Leonardo Borges is a programming languages enthusiast who loves writing code, contributing to open source software, and speaking on subjects he feels strongly about. After nearly 5 years of consulting at ThoughtWorks, where he worked in two commercial Clojure projects, among many others, he is now a software engineer at Atlassian. He uses Clojure and ClojureScript to help build real-time collaborative editing technology. This is his first full-length book, but he contributed a couple of chapters to *Clojure Cookbook*, *O'Reilly*.

Leonardo has founded and runs the Sydney Clojure User Group in Australia. He also writes posts about software, focusing on functional programming, on his website (`http://www.leonardoborges.com`). When he isn't writing code, he enjoys riding motorcycles, weightlifting, and playing the guitar.

Acknowledgments

I would like to take this opportunity and start by thanking my family: my grandparents, Altamir and Alba, for their tireless support; my mother, Sônia, for her unconditional love and motivation; and my uncle, Altamir Filho, for supporting me when I decided to go to school at night so that I could start working as a programmer. Without them, I would have never pursued software engineering.

I would also like to thank my fiancee, Enif, who answered with a resounding "yes" when asked whether I should take up the challenge of writing a book. Her patience, love, support, and words of encouragement were invaluable.

During the writing process, Packt Publishing involved several reviewers and their feedback was extremely useful in making this a better book. To these reviewers, thank you.

I am also sincerely grateful for my friends who provided crucial feedback on key chapters, encouraging me at every step of the way: Claudio Natoli, Fábio Lessa, Fabio Pereira, Julian Gamble, Steve Buikhuizen, and many others, who would take multiple pages to list.

Last but not least, a warm thanks to the staff at Packt Publishing, who helped me along the whole process, being firm and responsible, yet understanding.

Each of you helped make this happen. Thank you!

About the Reviewers

Eduard Bondarenko is a software developer living in Kiev, Ukraine. He started programming using Basic on ZXSpectrum a long time ago. Later, he worked in the web development domain.

He has used Ruby on Rails for about 8 years. Having used Ruby for a long time, he discovered Clojure in early 2009, and liked the language. Besides Ruby and Clojure, he is interested in Erlang, Go, Scala, and Haskell development.

Colin Jones is director of software services at 8th Light, where he builds web, mobile, and desktop systems for clients of all sizes. He's the author of *Mastering Clojure Macros: Write Cleaner, Faster, Smarter Code, Pragmatic Bookshelf*. Colin participates actively in the Clojure open source community, including work on the Clojure Koans, REPLy, leiningen, and makes small contributions to Clojure itself.

Michael Kohl has been developing with Ruby since 2004 and got acquainted with Clojure in 2009. He has worked as a systems administrator, journalist, systems engineer, German teacher, software developer, and penetration tester. He currently makes his living as a senior Ruby on Rails developer. He previously worked with Packt Publishing as a technical reviewer for *Ruby and MongoDB Web Development Beginner's Guide*.

Falko Riemenschneider started programming in 1989. In the last 15 years, he has worked on numerous Java Enterprise software projects for backends as well as frontends. He's especially interested in designing complex rich-user interfaces. In 2012, he noticed and learned Clojure. He quickly came in contact with ideas such as FRP and CSP that show great potential for a radically simpler UI architecture for desktop and in-browser clients.

Falko works for itemis, a Germany-based software consultancy firm with strong competence for language- and model-based software development. He cofounded a Clojure user group, and encourages other developers within and outside itemis to learn functional programming.

Falko posts regularly on http://www.falkoriemenschneider.de.

www.PacktPub.com

Support files, eBooks, discount offers, and more

For support files and downloads related to your book, please visit www.PacktPub.com.

Did you know that Packt offers eBook versions of every book published, with PDF and ePub files available? You can upgrade to the eBook version at www.PacktPub.com and as a print book customer, you are entitled to a discount on the eBook copy. Get in touch with us at service@packtpub.com for more details.

At www.PacktPub.com, you can also read a collection of free technical articles, sign up for a range of free newsletters and receive exclusive discounts and offers on Packt books and eBooks.

https://www2.packtpub.com/books/subscription/packtlib

Do you need instant solutions to your IT questions? PacktLib is Packt's online digital book library. Here, you can search, access, and read Packt's entire library of books.

Why subscribe?
- Fully searchable across every book published by Packt
- Copy and paste, print, and bookmark content
- On demand and accessible via a web browser

Free access for Packt account holders

If you have an account with Packt at www.PacktPub.com, you can use this to access PacktLib today and view 9 entirely free books. Simply use your login credentials for immediate access.

Table of Contents

Preface

Highly concurrent applications such as user interfaces have traditionally managed state through the mutation of global variables. Various actions are coordinated via event handlers, which are procedural in nature.

Over time, the complexity of a system increases. New feature requests come in, and it becomes harder and harder to reason about the application.

Functional programming presents itself as an extremely powerful ally in building reliable systems by eliminating mutable states and allowing applications to be written in a declarative and composable way.

Such principles gave rise to Functional Reactive Programming and Compositional Event Systems (CES), programming paradigms that are exceptionally useful in building asynchronous and concurrent applications. They allow you to model mutable states in a functional style.

This book is devoted to these ideas and presents a number of different tools and techniques to help manage the increasing complexity of modern systems.

What this book covers

Chapter 1, What is Reactive Programming?, starts by guiding you through a compelling example of a reactive application written in ClojureScript. It then takes you on a journey through the history of Reactive Programming, during which some important terminology is introduced, setting the tone for the following chapters.

Chapter 2, A Look at Reactive Extensions, explores the basics of this Reactive Programming framework. Its abstractions are introduced and important subjects such as error handling and back pressure are discussed.

Chapter 3, Asynchronous Programming and Networking, walks you through building a stock market application. It starts by using a more traditional approach and then switches to an implementation based on Reactive Extensions, examining the trade-offs between the two.

Chapter 4, Introduction to core.async, describes core.async, a library for asynchronous programming in Clojure. Here, you learn about the building blocks of Communicating Sequential Processes and how Reactive Applications are built with core.async.

Chapter 5, Creating Your Own CES Framework with core.async, embarks on the ambitious endeavor of building a CES framework. It leverages knowledge gained in the previous chapter and uses core.async as the foundation for the framework.

Chapter 6, Building a Simple ClojureScript Game with Reagi, showcases a domain where Reactive frameworks have been used for great effects in games development.

Chapter 7, The UI as a Function, shifts gears and shows how the principles of functional programming can be applied to web UI development through the lens of Om, a ClojureScript binding for Facebook's React.

Chapter 8, Futures, presents futures as a viable alternative to some classes' reactive applications. It examines the limitations of Clojure futures and presents an alternative: imminent, a library of composable futures for Clojure.

Chapter 9, A Reactive API to Amazon Web Services, describes a case study taken from a real project, where a lot of the concepts introduced throughout this book have been put together to interact with a third-party service.

Appendix A, The Algebra of Library Design, introduces concepts from Category Theory that are helpful in building reusable abstractions. The appendix is optional and won't hinder learning in the previous chapters. It presents the principles used in designing the futures library seen in *Chapter 8, Futures.*

Appendix B, Bibliography, provides all the references used throughout the book.

What you need for this book

This book assumes that you have a reasonably modern desktop or laptop computer as well as a working Clojure environment with leiningen (see http://leiningen. org/) properly configured.

Installation instructions depend on your platform and can be found on the leiningen website (see http://leiningen.org/#install).

You are free to use any text editor of your choice, but popular choices include Eclipse (see `https://eclipse.org/downloads/`) with the Counterclockwise plugin (see `https://github.com/laurentpetit/ccw`), IntelliJ (`https://www.jetbrains.com/idea/`) with the Cursive plugin (see `https://cursiveclojure.com/`), Light Table (see `http://lighttable.com/`), Emacs, and Vim.

Who this book is for

This book is for Clojure developers who are currently building or planning to build asynchronous and concurrent applications and who are interested in how they can apply the principles and tools of Reactive Programming to their daily jobs.

Knowledge of Clojure and leiningen—a popular Clojure build tool—is required.

The book also features several ClojureScript examples, and as such, familiarity with ClojureScript and web development in general will be helpful.

Notwithstanding, the chapters have been carefully written in such a way that as long as you possess knowledge of Clojure, following these examples should only require a little extra effort.

As this book progresses, it lays out the building blocks required by later chapters, and as such my recommendation is that you start with *Chapter 1, What is Reactive Programming?*, and work your way through subsequent chapters in order.

A clear exception to this is *Appendix A, The Algebra of Library Design*, which is optional and can be read independent of the others—although reading *Chapter 8, Futures*, might provide a useful background.

Conventions

In this book, you will find a number of styles of text that distinguish between different kinds of information. Here are some examples of these styles, and an explanation of their meaning.

Code words in text, database table names, folder names, filenames, file extensions, pathnames, dummy URLs, user input, and Twitter handles are shown as follows: "We can include other contexts through the use of the `include` directive."

A block of code is set as follows:

```
(def numbers (atom []))

(defn adder [key ref old-state new-state]
  (print "Current sum is " (reduce + new-state)))

(add-watch numbers :adder adder)
```

When we wish to draw your attention to a particular part of a code block, the relevant lines or items are set in bold:

```
(-> (repeat-obs 5)
    (rx/subscribe prn-to-repl))

;; 5
;; 5
```

Any command-line input or output is written as follows:

```
lein run -m sin-wave.server
```

New terms and **important words** are shown in bold. Words that you see on the screen, in menus, or dialog boxes, for example, appear in the text like this: "If this was a web application our users would be presented with a web server error such as the **HTTP code 500 – Internal Server Error**."

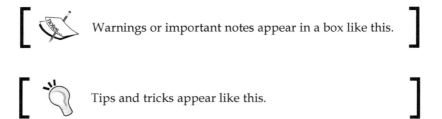

> Warnings or important notes appear in a box like this.

> Tips and tricks appear like this.

Reader feedback

Feedback from our readers is always welcome. Let us know what you think about this book — what you liked or may have disliked. Reader feedback is important for us to develop titles that you really get the most out of.

To send us general feedback, simply send an e-mail to feedback@packtpub.com, and mention the book title via the subject of your message.

If there is a topic that you have expertise in and you are interested in either writing or contributing to a book, see our author guide at www.packtpub.com/authors.

Customer support

Now that you are the proud owner of a Packt book, we have a number of things to help you to get the most from your purchase.

Downloading the example code

You can download the example code files for all Packt books you have purchased from your account at http://www.packtpub.com. If you purchased this book elsewhere, you can visit http://www.packtpub.com/support and register to have the files e-mailed directly to you.

Errata

Although we have taken every care to ensure the accuracy of our content, mistakes do happen. If you find a mistake in one of our books—maybe a mistake in the text or the code—we would be grateful if you would report this to us. By doing so, you can save other readers from frustration and help us improve subsequent versions of this book. If you find any errata, please report them by visiting http://www.packtpub.com/submit-errata, selecting your book, clicking on the **errata submission form** link, and entering the details of your errata. Once your errata are verified, your submission will be accepted and the errata will be uploaded on our website, or added to any list of existing errata, under the Errata section of that title. Any existing errata can be viewed by selecting your title from http://www.packtpub.com/support.

Piracy

Piracy of copyright material on the Internet is an ongoing problem across all media. At Packt, we take the protection of our copyright and licenses very seriously. If you come across any illegal copies of our works, in any form, on the Internet, please provide us with the location address or website name immediately so that we can pursue a remedy.

Please contact us at copyright@packtpub.com with a link to the suspected pirated material.

We appreciate your help in protecting our authors, and our ability to bring you valuable content.

Questions

You can contact us at questions@packtpub.com if you are having a problem with any aspect of this book, and we will do our best to address it.

1
What is Reactive Programming?

Reactive Programming is both an overloaded term and a broad topic. As such, this book will focus on a specific formulation of Reactive Programming called **Compositional Event Systems (CES)**.

Before covering some history and background behind Reactive Programming and CES, I would like to open with a working and hopefully compelling example: an animation in which we draw a sine wave onto a web page.

The sine wave is simply the graph representation of the sine function. It is a smooth, repetitive oscillation, and at the end of our animation it will look like the following screenshot:

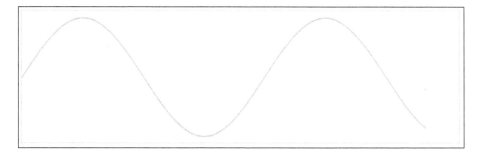

This example will highlight how CES:

- Urges us to think about *what* we would like to do as opposed to *how*
- Encourages small, specific abstractions that can be composed together
- Produces terse and maintainable code that is easy to change

The core of this program boils down to four lines of ClojureScript:

```
(-> sine-wave
    (.take 600)
    (.subscribe (fn [{:keys [x y]}]
                  (fill-rect x y "orange"))))
```

Simply by looking at this code it is impossible to determine precisely what it does. However, do take the time to read and imagine what it *could* do.

First, we have a variable called `sine-wave`, which represents the 2D coordinates we will draw onto the web page. The next line gives us the intuition that `sine-wave` is some sort of collection-like abstraction: we use `.take` to retrieve 600 coordinates from it.

Finally, we `.subscribe` to this "collection" by passing it a callback. This callback will be called for each item in the sine-wave, finally drawing at the given *x* and *y* coordinates using the `fill-rect` function.

This is quite a bit to take in for now as we haven't seen any other code yet—but that was the point of this little exercise: even though we know nothing about the specifics of this example, we are able to develop an intuition of how it might work.

Let's see what else is necessary to make this snippet animate a sine wave on our screen.

A taste of Reactive Programming

This example is built in ClojureScript and uses HTML 5 Canvas for rendering and RxJS (see `https://github.com/Reactive-Extensions/RxJS`)—a framework for Reactive Programming in JavaScript.

Before we start, keep in mind that we will not go into the details of these frameworks yet—that will happen later in this book. This means I'll be asking you to take quite a few things at face value, so don't worry if you don't immediately grasp how things work. The purpose of this example is to simply get us started in the world of Reactive Programming.

For this project, we will be using Chestnut (see `https://github.com/plexus/chestnut`)—a leiningen template for ClojureScript that gives us a sample working application we can use as a skeleton.

To create our new project, head over to the command line and invoke leiningen as follows:

```
lein new chestnut sin-wave
cd sin-wave
```

Next, we need to modify a couple of things in the generated project. Open up `sin-wave/resources/index.html` and update it to look like the following:

```
<!DOCTYPE html>
<html>
  <head>
    <link href="css/style.css" rel="stylesheet" type="text/css">
  </head>
  <body>
    <div id="app"></div>
    <script src="/js/rx.all.js" type="text/javascript"></script>
    <script src="/js/app.js" type="text/javascript"></script>
    <canvas id="myCanvas" width="650" height="200" style="border:1px
solid #d3d3d3;">
  </body>
</html>
```

This simply ensures that we import both our application code and RxJS. We haven't downloaded RxJS yet so let's do this now. Browse to `https://github.com/Reactive-Extensions/RxJS/blob/master/dist/rx.all.js` and save this file to `sin-wave/resources/public`. The previous snippets also add an HTML 5 Canvas element onto which we will be drawing.

Now, open `/src/cljs/sin_wave/core.cljs`. This is where our application code will live. You can ignore what is currently there. Make sure you have a clean slate like the following one:

```
(ns sin-wave.core)

(defn main [])
```

Finally, go back to the command line—under the `sin-wave` folder—and start up the following application:

```
lein run -m sin-wave.server
2015-01-02 19:52:34.116:INFO:oejs.Server:jetty-7.6.13.v20130916
2015-01-02 19:52:34.158:INFO:oejs.AbstractConnector:Started
SelectChannelConnector@0.0.0.0:10555
Starting figwheel.
Starting web server on port 10555 .
Compiling ClojureScript.
Figwheel: Starting server at http://localhost:3449
Figwheel: Serving files from '(dev-resources|resources)/public'
```

Once the previous command finishes, the application will be available at
`http://localhost:10555`, where you will find a blank, rectangular canvas.
We are now ready to begin.

The main reason we are using the Chestnut template for this example is that it
performs hot-reloading of our application code via websockets. This means we
can have the browser and the editor side by side, and as we update our code, we
will see the results immediately in the browser without having to reload the page.

To validate that this is working, open your web browser's console so that you can
see the output of the scripts in the page. Then add this to `/src/cljs/sin_wave/`
`core.cljs` as follows:

```
(.log js/console "hello clojurescript")
```

You should have seen the `hello clojurescript` message printed to your browser's
console. Make sure you have a working environment up to this point as we will be
relying on this workflow to interactively build our application.

It is also a good idea to make sure we clear the canvas every time Chestnut reloads
our file. This is simple enough to do by adding the following snippet to our core
namespace:

```
(def canvas (.getElementById js/document "myCanvas"))
(def ctx    (.getContext canvas "2d"))


;; Clear canvas before doing anything else
(.clearRect ctx 0 0 (.-width canvas) (.-height canvas))
```

Creating time

Now that we have a working environment, we can progress with our animation.
It is probably a good idea to specify how often we would like to have a new
animation frame.

This effectively means adding the concept of *time* to our application. You're free to
play with different values, but let's start with a new frame every 10 milliseconds:

```
(def interval   js/Rx.Observable.interval)
(def time       (interval 10))
```

As RxJS is a JavaScript library, we need to use ClojureScript's interoperability to call
its functions. For convenience, we bind the `interval` function of RxJS to a local var.
We will use this approach throughout this book when appropriate.

Next, we create an infinite stream of numbers — starting at 0 — that will have a new element every 10 milliseconds. Let's make sure this is working as expected:

```
(-> time
    (.take 5)
    (.subscribe (fn [n]
                  (.log js/console n)))))
;; 0
;; 1
;; 2
;; 3
;; 4
```

 I use the term *stream* very loosely here. It will be defined more precisely later in this book.

Remember time is infinite, so we use `.take` in order to avoid indefinitely printing out numbers to the console.

Our next step is to calculate the 2D coordinate representing a segment of the sine wave we can draw. This will be given by the following functions:

```
(defn deg-to-rad [n]
  (* (/ Math/PI 180) n))

(defn sine-coord [x]
  (let [sin (Math/sin (deg-to-rad x))
        y   (- 100 (* sin 90))]
    {:x   x
     :y   y
     :sin sin}))
```

The `sine-coord` function takes an x point of our 2D Canvas and calculates the y point based on the sine of x. The constants `100` and `90` simply control how tall and sharp the slope should be. As an example, try calculating the sine coordinate when x is 50:

```
(.log js/console (str (sine-coord 50)))
;;{:x 50, :y 31.05600011929198, :sin 0.766044443118978}
```

We will be using `time` as the source for the values of x. Creating the sine wave now is only a matter of combining both `time` and `sine-coord`:

```
(def sine-wave
  (.map time sine-coord))
```

Just like `time`, `sine-wave` is an infinite stream. The difference is that instead of just integers, we will now have the x and y coordinates of our sine wave, as demonstrated in the following:

```
(-> sine-wave
    (.take 5)
    (.subscribe (fn [xysin]
                  (.log js/console (str xysin)))))

;; {:x 0, :y 100, :sin 0}
;; {:x 1, :y 98.42928342064448, :sin 0.01745240643728351}
;; {:x 2, :y 96.85904529677491, :sin 0.03489949670250097}
;; {:x 3, :y 95.28976393813505, :sin 0.052335956242943835}
;; {:x 4, :y 93.72191736302872, :sin 0.0697564737441253}
```

This brings us to the original code snippet which piqued our interest, alongside a function to perform the actual drawing:

```
(defn fill-rect [x y colour]
  (set! (.-fillStyle ctx) colour)
  (.fillRect ctx x y 2 2))

(-> sine-wave
    (.take 600)
    (.subscribe (fn [{:keys [x y]}]
                  (fill-rect x y "orange"))))
```

As this point, we can save the file again and watch as the sine wave we have just created gracefully appears on the screen.

More colors

One of the points this example sets out to illustrate is how thinking in terms of very simple abstractions and then building more complex ones on top of them make for code that is simpler to maintain and easier to modify.

As such, we will now update our animation to draw the sine wave in different colors. In this case, we would like to draw the wave in red if the sine of x is negative and blue otherwise.

We already have the sine value coming through the `sine-wave` stream, so all we need to do is to transform this stream into one that will give us the colors according to the preceding criteria:

```
(def colour (.map sine-wave
                  (fn [{:keys [sin]}]
```

```
(if (< sin 0)
    "red"
    "blue"))))
```

The next step is to add the new stream into the main drawing loop—remember to comment the previous one so that we don't end up with multiple waves being drawn at the same time:

```
(-> (.zip sine-wave colour #(vector % %2))
    (.take 600)
    (.subscribe (fn [[{:keys [x y]} colour]]
                  (fill-rect x y colour))))
```

Once we save the file, we should see a new sine wave alternating between red and blue as the sine of x oscillates from –1 to 1.

Making it reactive

As fun as this has been so far, the animation we have created isn't really reactive. Sure, it does react to time itself, but that is the very nature of animation. As we will later see, Reactive Programming is so called because programs react to external inputs such as mouse or network events.

We will, therefore, update the animation so that the user is in control of when the color switch occurs: the wave will start red and switch to blue when the user clicks anywhere within the canvas area. Further clicks will simply alternate between red and blue.

We start by creating infinite—as per the definition of `time`—streams for our color primitives as follows:

```
(def red  (.map time (fn [_] "red")))
(def blue (.map time (fn [_] "blue")))
```

On their own, `red` and `blue` aren't that interesting as their values don't change. We can think of them as *constant* streams. They become a lot more interesting when combined with another infinite stream that cycles between them based on user input:

```
(def concat     js/Rx.Observable.concat)
(def defer      js/Rx.Observable.defer)
(def from-event js/Rx.Observable.fromEvent)


(def mouse-click (from-event canvas "click"))
```

```
(def cycle-colour
  (concat (.takeUntil red mouse-click)
          (defer #(concat (.takeUntil blue mouse-click)
                          cycle-colour))))
```

This is our most complex update so far. If you look closely, you will also notice that cycle-colour is a recursive stream; that is, it is defined in terms of itself.

When we first saw code of this nature, we took a leap of faith in trying to understand what it does. After a quick read, however, we realized that cycle-colour follows closely how we might have *talked* about the problem: we will use red until a mouse click occurs, after which we will use blue until another mouse click occurs. Then, we start the recursion.

The change to our animation loop is minimal:

```
(-> (.zip sine-wave cycle-colour #(vector % %2))
    (.take 600)
    (.subscribe (fn [[{:keys [x y]} colour]]
                  (fill-rect x y colour))))
```

The purpose of this book is to help you develop the instinct required to model problems in the way demonstrated here. After each chapter, more and more of this example will make sense. Additionally, a number of frameworks will be used both in ClojureScript and Clojure to give you a wide range of tools to choose from.

Before we move on to that, we must take a little detour and understand how we got here.

Exercise 1.1

Modify the previous example in such a way that the sine wave is drawn using all rainbow colors. The drawing loop should look like the following:

```
(-> (.zip sine-wave rainbow-colours #(vector % %2))
    (.take 600)
    (.subscribe (fn [[{:keys [x y]} colour]]
                  (fill-rect x y colour))))
```

Your task is to implement the rainbow-colours stream. As everything up until now has been very light on explanations, you might choose to come back to this exercise later, once we have covered more about CES.

The repeat, scan, and flatMap functions may be useful in solving this exercise. Be sure to consult RxJs' API at https://github.com/Reactive-Extensions/RxJS/blob/master/doc/libraries/rx.complete.md.

A bit of history

Before we talk about what Reactive Programming is, it is important to understand how other relevant programming paradigms influenced how we develop software. This will also help us understand the motivations behind reactive programming.

With few exceptions most of us have been taught—either self-taught or at school/university—imperative programming languages such as C and Pascal or object-oriented languages such as Java and C++.

In both cases, the imperative programming paradigm—of which object-oriented languages are part—dictates we write programs as a series of statements that modify program state.

In order to understand what this means, let's look at a short program written in pseudo-code that calculates the sum and the mean value of a list of numbers:

```
numbers := [1, 2, 3, 4, 5, 6]
sum := 0
for each number in numbers
  sum := sum + number
end
mean := sum / count(numbers)
```

The mean value is the average of the numbers in the list, obtained by dividing the sum by the number of elements.

First, we create a new array of integers, called numbers, with numbers from 1 to 6, inclusive. Then, we initialize sum to zero. Next, we iterate over the array of integers, one at a time, adding to sum the value of each number.

Lastly, we calculate and assign the average of the numbers in the list to the mean local variable. This concludes the program logic.

This program would print 21 for the sum and 3 for the mean, if executed.

Though a simple example, it highlights its imperative style: we set up an application state—sum—and then explicitly tell the computer how to modify that state in order to calculate the result.

Dataflow programming

The previous example has an interesting property: the value of mean clearly has a dependency on the contents of sum.

Dataflow programming makes this relationship explicit. It models applications as a dependency graph through which data flows—from operation to operation—and as values change, these changes are propagated to its dependencies.

Historically, dataflow programming has been supported by custom-built languages such as Lucid and BLODI, as such, leaving other general purpose programming languages out.

Let's see how this new insight would impact our previous example. We know that once the last line gets executed, the value of mean is assigned and won't change unless we explicitly reassign the variable.

However, let's imagine for a second that the pseudo-language we used earlier does support dataflow programming. In that case, assigning mean to an expression that refers to both sum and count, such as sum / count(numbers), would be enough to create the directed dependency graph in the following diagram:

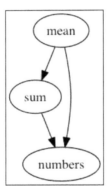

Note that a direct side effect of this relationship is that an implicit dependency from sum to numbers is also created. This means that if numbers change, the change is propagated through the graph, first updating sum and then finally updating mean.

This is where Reactive Programming comes in. This paradigm builds on dataflow programming and change propagation to bring this style of programming to languages that don't have native support for it.

For imperative programming languages, Reactive Programming can be made available via libraries or language extensions. We don't cover this approach in this book, but should the reader want more information on the subject, please refer to *dc-lib* (see https://code.google.com/p/dc-lib/) for an example. It is a framework that adds Reactive Programming support to C++ via dataflow constraints.

Object-oriented Reactive Programming

When designing interactive applications such as desktop **Graphical User Interfaces** (**GUIs**), we are essentially using an object-oriented approach to Reactive Programming. We will build a simple calculator application to demonstrate this style.

 Clojure isn't an object-oriented language, but we will be interacting with parts of the Java API to build user interfaces that were developed in an OO paradigm, hence the title of this section.

Let's start by creating a new leiningen project from the command line:

```
lein new calculator
```

This will create a directory called `calculator` in the current folder. Next, open the `project.clj` file in your favorite text editor and add a dependency on Seesaw, a Clojure library for working with Java Swing:

```
(defproject calculator "0.1.0-SNAPSHOT"
  :description "FIXME: write description"
  :url "http://example.com/FIXME"
  :license {:name "Eclipse Public License"
            :url "http://www.eclipse.org/legal/epl-v10.html"}
  :dependencies [[org.clojure/clojure "1.5.1"]
                 [seesaw "1.4.4"]])
```

At the time of this writing, the latest Seesaw version available is 1.4.4.

Next, in the `src/calculator/core.clj` file, we'll start by requiring the Seesaw library and creating the visual components we'll be using:

```
(ns calculator.core
  (:require [seesaw.core :refer :all]))

(native!)

(def main-frame (frame :title "Calculator" :on-close :exit))
```

```
(def field-x (text "1"))
(def field-y (text "2"))

(def result-label (label "Type numbers in the boxes to add them up!"))
```

The preceding snippet creates a window with the title `Calculator` that ends the program when closed. We also create two text input fields, `field-x` and `field-y`, as well as a label that will be used to display the results, aptly named `result-label`.

We would like the label to be updated automatically as soon as a user types a new number in any of the input fields. The following code does exactly that:

```
(defn update-sum [e]
  (try
    (text! result-label
         (str "Sum is " (+ (Integer/parseInt (text field-x))
                           (Integer/parseInt (text field-y)))))
    (catch Exception e
      (println "Error parsing input."))))

(listen field-x :key-released update-sum)
(listen field-y :key-released update-sum)
```

The first function, `update-sum`, is our event handler. It sets the text of `result-label` to the sum of the values in `field-x` and `field-y`. We use try/catch here as a really basic way to handle errors since the key pressed might not have been a number. We then add the event handler to the `:key-released` event of both input fields.

In real applications, we never want a catch block such as the previous one. This is considered bad style, and the catch block should do something more useful such as logging the exception, firing a notification, or resuming the application if possible.

We are almost done. All we need to do now is add the components we have created so far to our `main-frame` and finally display it as follows:

```
(config! main-frame :content
       (border-panel
         :north (horizontal-panel :items [field-x field-y])
         :center result-label
         :border 5))

(defn -main [& args]
  (-> main-frame pack! show!))
```

Now we can save the file and run the program from the command line in the project's root directory:

```
lein run -m calculator.core
```

You should see something like the following screenshot:

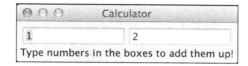

Experiment by typing some numbers in either or both text input fields and watch how the value of the label changes automatically, displaying the sum of both numbers.

Congratulations! You have just created your first reactive application!

As alluded to previously, this application is reactive because the value of the result label *reacts* to user input and is updated automatically. However, this isn't the whole story — it lacks in composability and requires us to specify the how, not the what of what we're trying to achieve.

As familiar as this style of programming may be, making applications reactive this way isn't always ideal.

Given previous discussions, we notice we still had to be fairly explicit in setting up the relationships between the various components as evidenced by having to write a custom handler and bind it to both input fields.

As we will see throughout the rest of this book, there is a much better way to handle similar scenarios.

The most widely used reactive program

Both examples in the previous section will feel familiar to some readers. If we call the input text fields "cells" and the result label's handler a "formula", we now have the nomenclature used in modern spreadsheet applications such as Microsoft Excel.

The term Reactive Programming has only been in use in recent years, but the idea of a reactive application isn't new. The first electronic spreadsheet dates back to 1969 when Rene Pardo and Remy Landau, then recent graduates from Harvard University, created **LANPAR (LANguage for Programming Arrays at Random)** [1].

It was invented to solve a problem that Bell Canada and AT&T had at the time: their budgeting forms had 2000 cells that, when modified, forced a software re-write taking anywhere from six months to two years.

To this day, electronic spreadsheets remain a powerful and useful tool for professionals of various fields.

The Observer design pattern

Another similarity the keen reader may have noticed is with the Observer design pattern. It is mainly used in object-oriented applications as a way for objects to communicate with each other without having any knowledge of who depends on its changes.

In Clojure, a simple version of the Observer pattern can be implemented using *watches*:

```
(def numbers (atom []))

(defn adder [key ref old-state new-state]
  (print "Current sum is " (reduce + new-state)))

(add-watch numbers :adder adder)
```

We start by creating our program state, in this case an atom holding an empty vector. Next, we create a watch function that knows how to sum all numbers in numbers. Finally, we add our watch function to the numbers atom under the :adder key (useful for removing watches).

The adder key conforms with the API contract required by add-watch and receives four arguments. In this example, we only care about new-state.

Now, whenever we update the value of numbers, its watch will be executed, as demonstrated in the following:

```
(swap! numbers conj 1)
;; Current sum is  1

(swap! numbers conj 2)
;; Current sum is  3

(swap! numbers conj 7)
;; Current sum is  10
```

The highlighted lines above indicate the result that is printed on the screen each time we update the atom.

Though useful, the Observer pattern still requires some amount of work in setting up the dependencies and the required program state in addition to being hard to compose.

That being said, this pattern has been extended and is at the core of one of the Reactive Programming frameworks we will look at later in this book, Microsoft's **Reactive Extensions (Rx)**.

Functional Reactive Programming

Just like Reactive Programming, **Functional Reactive Programming — FRP** for short — has unfortunately become an overloaded term.

Frameworks such as RxJava (see `https://github.com/ReactiveX/RxJava`), ReactiveCocoa (see `https://github.com/ReactiveCocoa/ReactiveCocoa`), and Bacon.js (see `https://baconjs.github.io/`) became extremely popular in recent years and had positioned themselves incorrectly as FRP libraries. This led to the confusion surrounding the terminology.

As we will see, these frameworks do not implement FRP but rather are inspired by it.

In the interest of using the correct terminology as well as understanding what "inspired by FRP" means, we will have a brief look at the different formulations of FRP.

Higher-order FRP

Higher-order FRP refers to the original research on FRP developed by Conal Elliott and Paul Hudak in their paper *Functional Reactive Animation* [2] from 1997. This paper presents *Fran*, a domain-specific language embedded in Haskell for creating reactive animations. It has since been implemented in several languages as a library as well as purpose built reactive languages.

If you recall the calculator example we created a few pages ago, we can see how that style of Reactive Programming requires us to manage state explicitly by directly reading and writing from/to the input fields. As Clojure developers, we know that avoiding state and mutable data is a good principle to keep in mind when building software. This principle is at the core of Functional Programming:

```
(->> [1 2 3 4 5 6]
     (map inc)
     (filter even?)
     (reduce +))
;; 12
```

This short program increments by one all elements in the original list, filters all even numbers, and adds them up using `reduce`.

Note how we didn't have to explicitly manage local state through at each step of the computation.

Differently from imperative programming, we focus on what we want to do, for example iteration, and not how we want it to be done, for example using a `for` loop. This is why the implementation matches our description of the program closely. This is known as declarative programming.

FRP brings the same philosophy to Reactive Programming. As the Haskell programming language wiki on the subject has wisely put it:

> *FRP is about handling time-varying values like they were regular values.*

Put another way, FRP is a declarative way of modeling systems that respond to input over time.

Both statements touch on the concept of time. We'll be exploring that in the next section, where we introduce the key abstractions provided by FRP: signals (or behaviors) and events.

Signals and events

So far we have been dealing with the idea of programs that react to user input. This is of course only a small subset of reactive systems but is enough for the purposes of this discussion.

User input happens several times through the execution of a program: key presses, mouse drags, and clicks are but a few examples of how a user might interact with our system. All these interactions happen over a period of time. FRP recognizes that time is an important aspect of reactive programs and makes it a first-class citizen through its abstractions.

Both signals (also called behaviors) and events are related to time. Signals represent continuous, time-varying values. Events, on the other hand, represent discrete occurrences at a given point in time.

For example, time is itself a signal. It varies continuously and indefinitely. On the other hand, a key press by a user is an event, a discrete occurrence.

It is important to note, however, that the semantics of how a signal changes need not be continuous. Imagine a signal that represents the current (x,y) coordinates of your mouse pointer.

This signal is said to change discretely as it depends on the user moving the mouse pointer — an event — which isn't a continuous action.

Implementation challenges

Perhaps the most defining characteristic of classical FRP is the use of continuous time.

This means FRP assumes that signals are changing all the time, even if their value is still the same, leading to needless recomputation. For example, the mouse position signal will trigger updates to the application dependency graph — like the one we saw previously for the mean program — even when the mouse is stationary.

Another problem is that classical FRP is synchronous by default: events are processed in order, one at a time. Harmless at first, this can cause delays, which would render an application unresponsive should an event take substantially longer to process.

Paul Hudak and others furthered research on higher-order FRP [7] [8] to address these issues, but that came at the cost of expressivity.

The other formulations of FRP aim to overcome these implementation challenges.

Throughout the rest of the chapter, I'll be using signals and behaviors interchangeably.

First-order FRP

The most well-known reactive language in this category is Elm (see `http://elm-lang.org/`), an FRP language that compiles to JavaScript. It was created by Evan Czaplicki and presented in his paper *Elm: Concurrent FRP for Functional GUIs* [3].

Elm makes some significant changes to higher-order FRP.

It abandons the idea of continuous time and is entirely event-driven. As a result, it solves the problem of needless recomputation highlighted earlier. First-order FRP combines both behaviors and events into signals which, in contrast to higher-order FRP, are discrete.

Additionally, first-order FRP allows the programmer to specify when synchronous processing of events isn't necessary, preventing unnecessary processing delays.

Finally, Elm is a strict programming language — meaning arguments to functions are evaluated eagerly — and that is a conscious decision as it prevents space and time leaks, which are possible in a lazy language such as Haskell.

In an FRP library such as Fran, implemented in a lazy language, memory usage can grow unwieldy as computations are deferred to the absolutely last possible moment, therefore causing a space leak. These larger computations, accumulated over time due to laziness, can then cause unexpected delays when finally executed, causing time leaks.

Asynchronous data flow

Asynchronous Data Flow generally refers to frameworks such as **Reactive Extensions (Rx)**, **ReactiveCocoa**, and **Bacon.js**. It is called as such as it completely eliminates synchronous updates.

These frameworks introduce the concept of **Observable Sequences** [4], sometimes called Event Streams.

This formulation of FRP has the advantage of not being confined to functional languages. Therefore, even imperative languages like Java can take advantage of this style of programming.

Arguably, these frameworks were responsible for the confusion around FRP terminology. Conal Elliott at some point suggested the term CES (see `https://twitter.com/conal/status/468875014461468677`).

I have since adopted this terminology (see `http://vimeo.com/100688924`) as I believe it highlights two important factors:

- A fundamental difference between CES and FRP: CES is entirely event-driven
- CES is highly composable via combinators, taking inspiration from FRP

CES is the main focus of this book.

Arrowized FRP

This is the last formulation we will look at. Arrowized FRP [5] introduces two main differences over higher-order FRP: it uses signal functions instead of signals and is built on top of John Hughes' Arrow combinators [6].

It is mostly about a different way of structuring code and can be implemented as a library. As an example, Elm supports Arrowized FRP via its Automaton (see `https://github.com/evancz/automaton`) library.

The first draft of this chapter grouped the different formulations of FRP under the broad categories of *Continuous and Discrete* FRP. Thanks to Evan Czaplicki's excellent talk *Controlling Time and Space: understanding the many formulations of FRP* (see https://www.youtube.com/watch?v=Agu6jipKfYw), I was able to borrow the more specific categories used here. These come in handy when discussing the different approaches to FRP.

Applications of FRP

The different FRP formulations are being used today in several problem spaces by professionals and big organizations alike. Throughout this book, we'll look at several examples of how CES can be applied. Some of these are interrelated as most modern programs have several cross-cutting concerns, but we will highlight two main areas.

Asynchronous programming and networking

GUIs are a great example of asynchronous programming. Once you open a web or a desktop application, it simply sits there, idle, waiting for user input.

This state is often called the event or main event loop. It is simply waiting for external stimuli, such as a key press, a mouse button click, new data from the network, or even a simple timer.

Each of these stimuli is associated with an event handler that gets called when one of these events happen, hence the asynchronous nature of GUI systems.

This is a style of programming we have been used to for many years, but as business and user needs grow, these applications grow in complexity as well, and better abstractions are needed to handle the dependencies between all the components of an application.

Another great example that deals with managing complexity around network traffic is Netflix, which uses CES to provide a reactive API to their backend services.

Complex GUIs and animations

Games are, perhaps, the best example of complex user interfaces as they have intricate requirements around user input and animations.

The Elm language we mentioned before is one of the most exciting efforts in building complex GUIs. Another example is Flapjax, also targeted at web applications, but is provided as a JavaScript library that can be integrated with existing JavaScript code bases.

Summary

Reactive Programming is all about building responsive applications. There are several ways in which we can make our applications reactive. Some are old ideas: dataflow programming, electronic spreadsheets, and the Observer pattern are all examples. But CES in particular has become popular in recent years.

CES aims to bring to Reactive Programming the declarative way of modeling problems that is at the core of Functional Programming. We should worry about what and not about how.

In next chapters, we will learn how we can apply CES to our own programs.

A Look at Reactive Extensions

2

Reactive Extensions — or Rx — is a Reactive Programming library from Microsoft to build complex asynchronous programs. It models time-varying values and events as observable sequences and is implemented by extending the Observer design pattern.

Its first target platform was .NET, but Netflix has ported Rx to the JVM under the name RxJava. Microsoft also develops and maintains a port of Rx to JavaScript called RxJS, which is the tool we used to build the sine-wave application. The two ports work a treat for us since Clojure runs on the JVM and ClojureScript in JavaScript environments.

As we saw in *Chapter 1, What is Reactive Programming?*, Rx is inspired by Functional Reactive Programming but uses different terminology. In FRP, the two main abstractions are behaviors and events. Although the implementation details are different, observable sequences represent events. Rx also provides a behavior-like abstraction through another data type called `BehaviorSubject`.

In this chapter, we will:

- Explore Rx's main abstraction: observables
- Learn about the duality between iterators and observables
- Create and manipulate observable sequences

The Observer pattern revisited

In *Chapter 1, What is Reactive Programming?*, we saw a brief overview of the Observer design pattern and a simple implementation of it in Clojure using watches. Here's how we did it:

```
(def numbers (atom []))

(defn adder [key ref old-state new-state]
```

```
    (print "Current sum is " (reduce + new-state)))

  (add-watch numbers :adder adder)
```

In the preceding example, our observable subject is the var, `numbers`. The observer is the `adder` watch. When the observable changes, it *pushes* its changes to the observer *synchronously*.

Now, contrast this to working with sequences:

```
(->> [1 2 3 4 5 6]
     (map inc)
     (filter even?)
     (reduce +))
```

This time around, the vector is the subject being observed and the functions processing it can be thought of as the observers. However, this works in a pull-based model. The vector doesn't push any elements down the sequence. Instead, `map` and friends ask the sequence for more elements. This is a synchronous operation.

Rx makes sequences — and more — behave like observables so that you can still map, filter, and compose them just as you would compose functions over normal sequences.

Observer – an Iterator's dual

Clojure's sequence operators such as map, filter, reduce, and so on support Java Iterables. As the name implies, an Iterable is an object that can be iterated over. At a low level, this is supported by retrieving an Iterator reference from such object. Java's Iterator interface looks like the following:

```
public interface Iterator<E> {
    boolean hasNext();
    E next();
    void remove();
}
```

When passed in an object that implements this interface, Clojure's sequence operators pull data from it by using the `next` method, while using the `hasNext` method to know when to stop.

The `remove` method is required to remove its last element from the underlying collection. This in-place mutation is clearly unsafe in a multithreaded environment. Whenever Clojure implements this interface for the purposes of interoperability, the `remove` method simply throws `UnsupportedOperationException`.

An observable, on the other hand, has observers subscribed to it. Observers have the following interface:

```
public interface Observer<T> {
    void onCompleted();
    void onError(Throwable e);
    void onNext(T t);
}
```

As we can see, an Observer implementing this interface will have its onNext method called with the next value available from whatever observable it's subscribed to. Hence, it being a *push*-based notification model.

This duality [4] becomes clearer if we look at both the interfaces side by side:

```
Iterator<E> {                    Observer<T> {
    boolean hasNext();               void onCompleted();
    E next();                        void onError(Throwable e);
    void remove();                   void onNext(T t);
}                                }
```

Observables provide the ability to have producers push items *asynchronously* to consumers. A few examples will help solidify our understanding.

Creating Observables

This chapter is all about Reactive Extensions, so let's go ahead and create a project called rx-playground that we will be using in our exploratory tour. We will use RxClojure (see https://github.com/ReactiveX/RxClojure), a library that provides Clojure bindings for RxJava() (see https://github.com/ReactiveX/RxJava):

$ lein new rx-playground

Open the project file and add a dependency on RxJava's Clojure bindings:

```
(defproject rx-playground "0.1.0-SNAPSHOT"
  :description "FIXME: write description"
  :url "http://example.com/FIXME"
  :license {:name "Eclipse Public License"
            :url "http://www.eclipse.org/legal/epl-v10.html"}
  :dependencies [[org.clojure/clojure "1.5.1"]
                 [io.reactivex/rxclojure "1.0.0"]])"]])
```

Now, fire up a REPL in the project's root directory so that we can start creating some observables:

```
$ lein repl
```

The first thing we need to do is import RxClojure, so let's get this out of the way by typing the following in the REPL:

```
(require '[rx.lang.clojure.core :as rx])
(import '(rx Observable))
```

The simplest way to create a new observable is by calling the justreturn function:

```
(def obs (rx/return 10))
```

Now, we can subscribe to it:

```
(rx/subscribe obs
              (fn [value]
                (prn (str "Got value: " value))))
```

This will print the string "Got value: 10" to the REPL.

The subscribe function of an observable allows us to register handlers for three main things that happen throughout its life cycle: new values, errors, or a notification that the observable is done emitting values. This corresponds to the onNext, onError, and onCompleted methods of the Observer interface, respectively.

In the preceding example, we are simply subscribing to onNext, which is why we get notified about the observable's only value, 10.

A single-value Observable isn't terribly interesting though. Let's create and interact with one that emits multiple values:

```
(-> (rx/seq->o [1 2 3 4 5 6 7 8 9 10])
    (rx/subscribe prn))
```

This will print the numbers from 1 to 10, inclusive, to the REPL. seq->o is a way to create observables from Clojure sequences. It just so happens that the preceding snippet can be rewritten using Rx's own range operator:

```
(-> (rx/range 1 10)
    (rx/subscribe prn))
```

Of course, this doesn't yet present any advantages to working with raw values or sequences in Clojure.

But what if we need an observable that emits an undefined number of integers at a given interval? This becomes challenging to represent as a sequence in Clojure, but Rx makes it trivial:

```
(import '(java.util.concurrent TimeUnit))
(rx/subscribe (Observable/interval 100 TimeUnit/MILLISECONDS)
              prn-to-repl)
```

 RxClojure doesn't yet provide bindings to all of RxJava's API. The `interval` method is one such example. We're required to use interoperability and call the method directly on the `Observable` class from RxJava.

Observable/interval takes as arguments a number and a time unit. In this case, we are telling it to emit an integer — starting from zero — every 100 milliseconds. If we type this in an REPL-connected editor, however, two things will happen:

- We will not see any output (depending on your REPL; this is true for Emacs)
- We will have a rogue thread emitting numbers indefinitely

Both issues arise from the fact that `Observable/interval` is the first factory method we have used that doesn't emit values synchronously. Instead, it returns an Observable that defers the work to a separate thread.

The first issue is simple enough to fix. Functions such as `prn` will print to whatever the dynamic var `*out*` is bound to. When working in certain REPL environments such as Emacs', this is bound to the REPL stream, which is why we can generally see everything we print.

However, since Rx is deferring the work to a separate thread, `*out*` isn't bound to the REPL stream anymore so we don't see the output. In order to fix this, we need to capture the current value of `*out*` and bind it in our subscription. This will be incredibly useful as we experiment with Rx in the REPL. As such, let's create a helper function for it:

```
(def  repl-out *out*)
(defn prn-to-repl [& args]
  (binding [*out* repl-out]
    (apply prn args)))
```

The first thing we do is create a var `repl-out` that contains the current REPL stream. Next, we create a function `prn-to-repl` that works just like `prn`, except it uses the `binding` macro to create a new binding for `*out*` that is valid within that scope.

This still leaves us with the rogue thread problem. Now is the appropriate time to mention that the `subscribe` method from an Observable returns a subscription object. By holding onto a reference to it, we can call its `unsubscribe` method to indicate that we are no longer interested in the values produced by that observable.

Putting it all together, our interval example can be rewritten like the following:

```
(def subscription (rx/subscribe (Observable/interval 100 TimeUnit/
MILLISECONDS)
                                       prn-to-repl))

(Thread/sleep 1000)

(rx/unsubscribe subscription)
```

We create a new interval observable and immediately subscribe to it, just as we did before. This time, however, we assign the resulting subscription to a local var. Note that it now uses our helper function `prn-to-repl`, so we will start seeing values being printed to the REPL straight away.

Next, we sleep the current—the REPL—thread for a second. This is enough time for the Observable to produce numbers from 0 to 9. That's roughly when the REPL thread wakes up and unsubscribes from that observable, causing it to stop emitting values.

Custom Observables

Rx provides many more factory methods to create Observables (see `https://github.com/ReactiveX/RxJava/wiki/Creating-Observables`), but it is beyond the scope of this book to cover them all.

Nevertheless, sometimes, none of the built-in factories is what you want. For such cases, Rx provides the `create` method. We can use it to create a custom observable from scratch.

As an example, we'll create our own version of the just observable we used earlier in this chapter:

```
(defn just-obs [v]
  (rx/observable*
   (fn [observer]
     (rx/on-next observer v)
```

```
        (rx/on-completed observer)))))

    (rx/subscribe (just-obs 20) prn)
```

First, we create a function, `just-obs`, which implements our observable by calling the `observable*` function.

When creating an observable this way, the function passed to `observable*` will get called with an observer as soon as one subscribes to us. When this happens, we are free to do whatever computation—and even I/O—we need in order to produce values and push them to the observer.

We should remember to call the observer's `onCompleted` method whenever we're done producing values. The preceding snippet will print 20 to the REPL.

[While creating custom observables is fairly straightforward, we should make sure we exhaust the built-in factory functions first, only then resorting to creating our own.]

Manipulating Observables

Now that we know how to create observables, we should look at what kinds of interesting things we can do with them. In this section, we will see what it means to treat Observables as sequences.

We'll start with something simple. Let's print the sum of the first five positive even integers from an observable of all integers:

```
(rx/subscribe (->> (Observable/interval 1 TimeUnit/MICROSECONDS)
                   (rx/filter even?)
                   (rx/take 5)
                   (rx/reduce +))
              prn-to-repl)
```

This is starting to look awfully familiar to us. We create an interval that will emit all positive integers starting at zero every 1 microsecond. Then, we filter all even numbers in this observable. Obviously, this is too big a list to handle, so we simply take the first five elements from it. Finally, we reduce the value using +. The result is 20.

To drive home the point that programming with observables really is just like operating on sequences, we will look at one more example where we will combine two different Observable sequences. One contains the names of musicians I'm a fan of and the other the names of their respective bands:

```
(defn musicians []
  (rx/seq->o ["James Hetfield" "Dave Mustaine" "Kerry King"]))

(defn bands     []
  (rx/seq->o ["Metallica" "Megadeth" "Slayer"]))
```

We would like to print to the REPL a string of the format Musician name - from: band name. An added requirement is that the band names should be printed in uppercase for impact.

We'll start by creating another observable that contains the uppercased band names:

```
(defn uppercased-obs []
  (rx/map (fn [s] (.toUpperCase s)) (bands)))
```

While not strictly necessary, this makes a reusable piece of code that can be handy in several places of the program, thus avoiding duplication. Subscribers interested in the original band names can keep subscribing to the bands observable.

With the two observables in hand, we can proceed to combine them:

```
(-> (rx/map vector
            (musicians)
            (uppercased-obs))
    (rx/subscribe (fn [[musician band]]
                    (prn-to-repl (str musician " - from: " band)))))
```

Once more, this example should feel familiar. The solution we were after was a way to zip the two observables together. RxClojure provides zip behavior through map, much like Clojure's core map function does. We call it with three arguments: the two observables to zip and a function that will be called with both elements, one from each observable, and should return an appropriate representation. In this case, we simply turn them into a vector.

Next, in our subscriber, we simply destructure the vector in order to access the musician and band names. We can finally print the final result to the REPL:

```
"James Hetfield - from: METALLICA"

"Dave Mustaine - from: MEGADETH"

"Kerry King - from: SLAYER"
```

Flatmap and friends

In the previous section, we learned how to transform and combine observables with operations such as map, reduce, and `zip`. However, the two observables above — musicians and bands — were perfectly capable of producing values on their own. They did not need any extra input.

In this section, we examine a different scenario: we'll learn how we can combine observables, where the output of one is the input of another. We encountered `flatmap` before in *Chapter 1, What is Reactive Programming?* If you have been wondering what its role is, this section addresses exactly that.

Here's what we are going to do: given an observable representing a list of all positive integers, we'll calculate the factorial for all even numbers in that list. Since the list is too big, we'll take five items from it. The end result should be the factorials of 0, 2, 4, 6, and 8, respectively.

The first thing we need is a function to calculate the factorial of a number *n*, as well as our observable:

```
(defn factorial [n]
  (reduce * (range 1 (inc n))))

(defn all-positive-integers []
  (Observable/interval 1 TimeUnit/MICROSECONDS))
```

Using some type of visual aid will be helpful in this section, so we'll start with a marble diagram representing the previous observable:

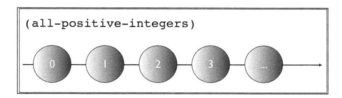

The middle arrow represents time and it flows from left to right. This diagram represents an infinite Observable sequence, as indicated by the use of ellipsis at the end of it.

Since we're combining all the observables now, we'll create one that, given a number, emits its factorial using the helper function defined earlier. We'll use Rx's `create` method for this purpose:

```
(defn fact-obs [n]
  (rx/observable*
```

```
(fn [observer]
  (rx/on-next observer (factorial n))
  (rx/on-completed observer)))))
```

This is very similar to the just-obs observable we created earlier in this chapter, except that it calculates the factorial of its argument and emits the result/factorial instead, ending the sequence immediately thereafter. The following diagram illustrates how it works:

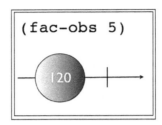

We feed the number 5 to the observable, which in turn emits its factorial, 120. The vertical bar at the end of the time line indicates the sequence terminates then.

Running the code confirms that our function is correct:

```
(rx/subscribe (fact-obs 5) prn-to-repl)
```

```
;; 120
```

So far so good. Now, we need to combine both observables in order to achieve our goal. This is where flatmap of Rx comes in. We'll first see it in action and then get into the explanation:

```
(rx/subscribe (->> (all-positive-integers)
                   (rx/filter  even?)
                   (rx/flatmap fact-obs)
                   (rx/take 5))
              prn-to-repl)
```

If we run the preceding code, it will print the factorials for 0, 2, 4, 6, and 8, just like we wanted:

```
1
2
24
720
40320
```

Most of the preceding code snippet should look familiar. The first thing we do is filter all even numbers from `all-positive-numbers`. This leaves us with the following observable sequence:

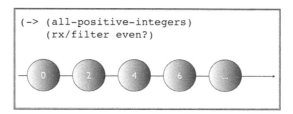

Much like `all-positive-integers`, this, too, is an infinite observable.

However, the next line of our code looks a little odd. We call `flatmap` and give it the `fact-obs` function. A function we know itself returns another observable. `flatmap` will call `fact-obs` with each value it emits. `fact-obs` will, in turn, return a single-value observable for each number. However, our subscriber doesn't know how to deal with observables! It's simply interested in the factorials!

This is why, after calling `fact-obs` to obtain an observable, `flatmap` flattens all of them into a single observable we can subscribe to. This is quite a mouthful, so let's visualize what this means:

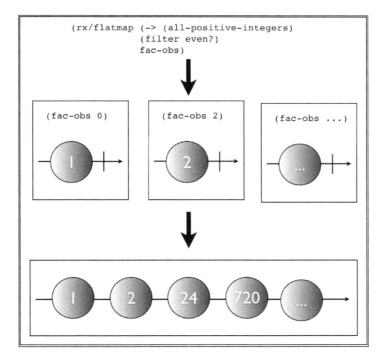

As you can see in the preceding diagram, throughout the execution of flatmap, we end up with a list of observables. However, we don't care about each observable but rather about the values they emit. Flatmap, then, is the perfect tool as it combines — *flattens* — all of them into the observable sequence shown at the bottom of the figure.

You can think of flatmap as *mapcat* for observable sequences.

The rest of the code is straightforward. We simply take the first five elements from this observable and subscribe to it, as we have been doing so far.

One more flatmap for the road

You might be wondering what would happen if the observable sequence we're *flatmapping* emitted more than one value. What then?

We'll see one last example before we begin the next section in order to illustrate the behavior of flatMap in such cases.

Here's an observable that emits its argument twice:

```
(defn repeat-obs [n]
  (rx/seq->o (repeat 2 n)))
```

Using it is straightforward:

```
(-> (repeat-obs 5)
    (rx/subscribe prn-to-repl))

;; 5
;; 5
```

As previously, we'll now combine this observable with the one we created earlier, all-positive-integers. Before reading on, think about what you expect the output to be for, say, the first three positive integers.

The code is as follows:

```
(rx/subscribe (->> (all-positive-integers)
                   (rx/flatmap repeat-obs)
                   (rx/take 6))
              prn-to-repl)
```

And the output is as follows:

```
0
0
1
```

1
2
2

The result might be unexpected for some readers. Let's have a look at the marble diagram for this example and make sure we understand how it works:

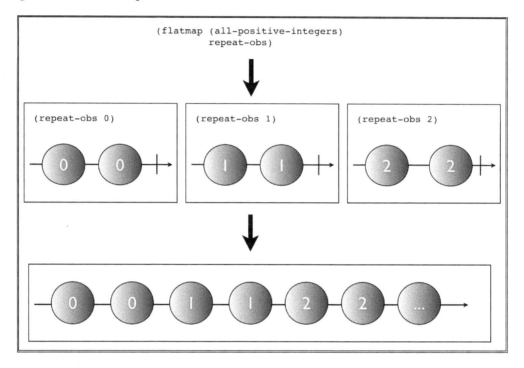

Each time `repeat-obs` gets called, it emits two values and terminates. `flatmap` then combines them all in a single observable, making the previous output clearer.

One last thing worth mentioning about `flatmap` — and the title of this section — is that its "friends" refer to the several names by which `flatmap` is known.

For instance, Rx.NET calls it `selectMany`. RxJava and Scala call it `flatMap` — though RxJava has an alias for it called `mapMany`. The Haskell community calls it *bind*. Though they have different names, these functions semantics are the same and are part of a higher-order abstraction called a Monad. We don't need to know anything about Monads to proceed.

The important thing to keep in mind is that when you're sitting at the bar talking to your friends about **Compositional Event Systems**, all these names mean the same thing.

Error handling

A very important aspect of building reliable applications is knowing what to do when things go wrong. It is naive to assume that the network is reliable, that hardware won't fail, or that we, as developers, won't make mistakes.

RxJava embraces this fact and provides a rich set of combinators to deal with failure, a few of which we examine here.

OnError

Let's get started by creating a badly behaved observable that always throws an exception:

```
(defn exceptional-obs []
  (rx/observable*
   (fn [observer]
     (rx/on-next observer (throw (Exception. "Oops. Something went
wrong")))
     (rx/on-completed observer))))
```

Now let's watch what happens if we subscribe to it:

```
(rx/subscribe (->> (exceptional-obs)
                   (rx/map inc))
              (fn [v] (prn-to-repl "result is " v)))

;; Exception Oops. Something went wrong  rx-playground.core/
exceptional-obs/fn--1505
```

The exception thrown by `exceptional-obs` isn't caught anywhere so it simply bubbles up to the REPL. If this was a web application our users would be presented with a web server error such as the **HTTP code 500 – Internal Server Error**. Those users would probably not use our system again.

Ideally, we would like to get a chance to handle this exception gracefully, possibly rendering a friendly error message that will let ours users know we care about them.

As we have seen earlier in the chapter, the `subscribe` function can take up to 3 functions as arguments:

- The first, or the `onNext` handler, is called when the observable emits a new value
- The second, or `onError`, is called whenever the observable throws an exception

- The third and last function, or `onComplete`, is called when the observable has completed and will not emit any new items

For our purposes we are interested in the `onError` handler, and using it is straightforward:

```
(rx/subscribe (->> (exceptional-obs)
                   (rx/map inc))
              (fn [v] (prn-to-repl "result is " v))
              (fn [e] (prn-to-repl "error is " e)))

;; "error is " #<Exception java.lang.Exception: Oops. Something went
wrong>
```

This time, instead of throwing the exception, our error handler gets called with it. This gives us the opportunity to display an appropriate message to our users.

Catch

The use of `onError` gives us a much better experience overall but it isn't very flexible.

Let's imagine a different scenario where we have an observable retrieving data from the network. What if, when this observer fails, we would like to present the user with a cached value instead of an error message?

This is where the `catch` combinator comes in. It allows us to specify a function to be invoked when the observable throws an exception, much like `OnError` does.

Differently from `OnError`, however, `catch` has to return a new Observable that will be the new source of items from the moment the exception was thrown:

```
(rx/subscribe (->> (exceptional-obs)
                   (rx/catch Exception e
                       (rx/return 10))
                   (rx/map inc))
              (fn [v] (prn-to-repl "result is " v)))

;; "result is " 11
```

In the previous example, we are essentially specifying that, whenever `exceptional-obs` throws, we should return the value `10`. We are not limited to single values, however. In fact, we can use any Observable we like as the new source:

```
(rx/subscribe (->> (exceptional-obs)
                   (rx/catch Exception e
                       (rx/seq->o (range 5)))
```

```
                       (rx/map inc))
          (fn [v] (prn-to-repl "result is " v)))
```

```
;; "result is " 1
;; "result is " 2
;; "result is " 3
;; "result is " 4
;; "result is " 5
```

Retry

The last error handling combinator we'll examine is `retry`. This combinator is useful when we know an error or exception is only transient so we should probably give it another shot by resubscribing to the Observable.

First, we'll create an observable that fails when it is subscribed to for the first time. However, the next time it is subscribed to, it succeeds and emits a new item:

```
(defn retry-obs []
  (let [errored (atom false)]
    (rx/observable*
     (fn [observer]
       (if @errored
         (rx/on-next observer 20)
         (do (reset! errored true)
             (throw (Exception. "Oops. Something went wrong"))))))))
```

Let's see what happens if we simply subscribe to it:

```
(rx/subscribe (retry-obs)
              (fn [v] (prn-to-repl "result is " v)))
```

```
;; Exception Oops. Something went wrong  rx-playground.core/retry-obs/
fn--1476
```

As expected, the exception simply bubbles up as in our first example. However we know — for the purposes of this example — that this is a transient failure. Let's see what changes if we use `retry`:

```
(rx/subscribe (->> (retry-obs)
                   (.retry))
              (fn [v] (prn-to-repl "result is " v)))
```

```
;; "result is " 20
```

Now, our code is responsible for retrying the Observable and as expected we get the correct output.

It's important to note that `retry` will attempt to resubscribe indefinitely until it succeeds. This might not be what you want so Rx provides a variation, called `retryWith`, which allows us to specify a predicate function that controls when and if retrying should stop.

All these operators give us the tools we need to build reliable reactive applications and we should always keep them in mind as they are, without a doubt, a great addition to our toolbox. The RxJava wiki on the subject should be referred to for more information: `https://github.com/ReactiveX/RxJava/wiki/Error-Handling-Operators`.

Backpressure

Another issue we might be faced with is the one of observables that produce items faster than we can consume. The problem that arises in this scenario is what to do with this ever-growing backlog of items.

As an example, think about zipping two observables together. The `zip` operator (or `map` in RxClojure) will only emit a new value when all observables have emitted an item.

So if one of these observables is a lot faster at producing items than the others, `map` will need to buffer these items and wait for the others, which will most likely cause an error, as shown here:

```
(defn fast-producing-obs []
  (rx/map inc (Observable/interval 1 TimeUnit/MILLISECONDS)))

(defn slow-producing-obs []
  (rx/map inc (Observable/interval 500 TimeUnit/MILLISECONDS)))

(rx/subscribe (->> (rx/map vector
                          (fast-producing-obs)
                          (slow-producing-obs))
                   (rx/map (fn [[x y]]
                             (+ x y)))
                   (rx/take 10))
              prn-to-repl
              (fn [e] (prn-to-repl "error is " e)))

;; "error is " #<MissingBackpressureException rx.exceptions.
MissingBackpressureException>
```

As seen in the preceding code, we have a fast producing observable that emits items 500 times faster than the slower Observable. Clearly, we can't keep up with it and surely enough, Rx throws `MissingBackpressureException`.

What this exception is telling us is that the fast producing observable doesn't support any type of backpressure — what Rx calls *Reactive pull backpressure* — that is, consumers can't tell it to go slower. Thankfully Rx provides us with combinators that are helpful in these scenarios.

Sample

One such combinator is `sample`, which allows us to sample an observable at a given interval, thus throttling the source observable's output. Let's apply it to our previous example:

```
(rx/subscribe (->> (rx/map vector
                           (.sample (fast-producing-obs) 200
                                    TimeUnit/MILLISECONDS)
                           (slow-producing-obs))
                    (rx/map (fn [[x y]]
                              (+ x y)))
                    (rx/take 10))
              prn-to-repl
              (fn [e] (prn-to-repl "error is " e)))

;; 204
;; 404
;; 604
;; 807
;; 1010
;; 1206
;; 1407
;; 1613
;; 1813
;; 2012
```

The only change is that we call `sample` on our fast producing Observable before calling `map`. We will sample it every 200 milliseconds.

By ignoring all other items emitted in this time slice, we have mitigated our initial problem, even though the original Observable doesn't support any form of backpressure.

The sample combinator is only one of the combinators useful in such cases. Others include `throttleFirst`, `debounce`, `buffer`, and `window`. One drawback of this approach, however, is that a lot of the items generated end up being ignored.

Depending on the type of application we are building, this might be an acceptable compromise. But what if we are interested in all items?

Backpressure strategies

If an Observable doesn't support backpressure but we are still interested in all items it emits, we can use one of the built-in backpressure combinators provided by Rx.

As an example we will look at one such combinator, `onBackpressureBuffer`:

```
(rx/subscribe (->> (rx/map vector
                        (.onBackpressureBuffer (fast-producing-
obs))
                        (slow-producing-obs))
                (rx/map (fn [[x y]]
                        (+ x y)))
                (rx/take 10))
            prn-to-repl
            (fn [e] (prn-to-repl "error is " e)))

;; 2
;; 4
;; 6
;; 8
;; 10
;; 12
;; 14
;; 16
;; 18
;; 20
```

The example is very similar to the one where we used `sample`, but the output is fairly different. This time we get all items emitted by both observables.

The `onBackpressureBuffer` strategy implements a strategy that simply buffers all items emitted by the slower Observable, emitting them whenever the consumer is ready. In our case, that happens every 500 milliseconds.

Other strategies include `onBackpressureDrop` and `onBackpressureBlock`.

It's worth noting that Reactive pull backpressure is still work in progress and the best way to keep up to date with progress is on the RxJava wiki on the subject: `https://github.com/ReactiveX/RxJava/wiki/Backpressure`.

Summary

In this chapter, we took a deep dive into RxJava, a port form Microsoft's Reactive Extensions from .NET. We learned about its main abstraction, the observable, and how it relates to iterables.

We also learned how to create, manipulate, and combine observables in several ways. The examples shown here were contrived to keep things simple. Nevertheless, all concepts presented are extremely useful in real applications and will come in handy for our next chapter, where we put them to use in a more substantial example.

Finally, we finished by looking at error handling and backpressure, both of which are important characteristics of reliable applications that should always be kept in mind.

3
Asynchronous Programming and Networking

Several business applications need to react to external stimuli—such as network traffic—asynchronously. An example of such software might be a desktop application that allows us to track a company's share prices in the stock market.

We will build this application first using a more traditional approach. In doing so, we will:

- Be able to identify and understand the drawbacks of the first design
- Learn how to use RxClojure to deal with stateful computations such as rolling averages
- Rewrite the example in a declarative fashion using observable sequences, thus reducing the complexity found in our first approach

Building a stock market monitoring application

Our stock market program will consist of three main components:

- A function simulating an external service from which we can query the current price—this would likely be a network call in a real setting
- A scheduler that polls the preceding function at a predefined interval
- A display function responsible for updating the screen

We'll start by creating a new leiningen project, where the source code for our application will live. Type the following on the command line and then switch into the newly created directory:

```
lein new stock-market-monitor
cd stock-market-monitor
```

As we'll be building a GUI for this application, go ahead and add a dependency on Seesaw to the dependencies section of your project.clj:

```
[seesaw "1.4.4"]
```

Next, create a src/stock_market_monitor/core.clj file in your favorite editor. Let's create and configure our application's UI components:

```
(ns stock-market-monitor.core
  (:require [seesaw.core :refer :all])
  (:import (java.util.concurrent ScheduledThreadPoolExecutor
                                 TimeUnit)))

(native!)

(def main-frame (frame :title "Stock price monitor"
                       :width 200 :height 100
                       :on-close :exit))

(def price-label      (label "Price: -"))

(config! main-frame :content price-label)
```

As you can see, the UI is fairly simple. It consists of a single label that will display a company's share price. We also imported two Java classes, ScheduledThreadPoolExecutor and TimeUnit, which we will use shortly.

The next thing we need is our polling machinery so that we can invoke the pricing service on a given schedule. We'll implement this via a thread pool so as not to block the main thread:

 User interface SDKs such as swing have the concept of a main — or UI — thread. This is the thread used by the SDK to render the UI components to the screen. As such, if we have blocking — or even simply slow running — operations execute in this thread, the user experience will be severely affected, hence the use of a thread pool to offload expensive function calls.

```
(def pool (atom nil))

(defn init-scheduler [num-threads]
```

```
     (reset! pool  (ScheduledThreadPoolExecutor. num-threads))))
(defn run-every [pool millis f]
  (.scheduleWithFixedDelay pool
                           f
                           0 millis TimeUnit/MILLISECONDS))

(defn shutdown [pool]
  (println "Shutting down scheduler...")
  (.shutdown pool))
```

The `init-scheduler` function creates `ScheduledThreadPoolExecutor` with the given number of threads. That's the thread pool in which our periodic function will run. The `run-every` function schedules a function `f` in the given `pool` to run at the interval specified by `millis`. Finally, `shutdown` is a function that will be called on program termination and shutdown the thread pool gracefully.

The rest of the program puts all these parts together:

```
(defn share-price [company-code]
  (Thread/sleep 200)
  (rand-int 1000))


(defn -main [& args]
  (show! main-frame)
  (.addShutdownHook (Runtime/getRuntime)
                    (Thread. #(shutdown @pool)))
  (init-scheduler 1)
  (run-every @pool 500
             #(->> (str "Price: " (share-price "XYZ"))
                   (text! price-label)
                   invoke-now)))
```

The `share-price` function sleeps for 200 milliseconds to simulate network latency and returns a random integer between 0 and 1,000 representing the stock's price.

The first line of our `-main` function adds a shutdown hook to the runtime. This allows our program to intercept termination—such as pressing *Ctrl + C* in a terminal window—and gives us the opportunity to shutdown the thread pool.

The `ScheduledThreadPoolExecutor` pool creates non-daemon threads by default. A program cannot terminate if there are any non-daemon threads alive in addition to the program's main thread. This is why the shutdown hook is necessary.

Next, we initialize the scheduler with a single thread and schedule a function to be executed every 500 milliseconds. This function asks the `share-price` function for XYZ's current price and updates the label.

 Desktop applications require all rendering to be done in the UI thread. However, our periodic function runs on a separate thread and needs to update the price label. This is why we use `invoke-now`, which is a Seesaw function that schedules its body to be executed in the UI thread as soon as possible.

Let's run the program by typing the following command in the project's root directory:

```
lein trampoline run -m stock-market-monitor.core
```

 Trampolining tells leiningen not to nest our program's JVM within its own, thus freeing us to handle uses of *Ctrl + C* ourselves through shutdown hooks.

A window like the one shown in the following screenshot will be displayed, with the values on it being updated as per the schedule implemented earlier:

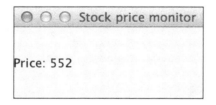

This is a fine solution. The code is relatively straightforward and satisfies our original requirements. However, if we look at the big picture, there is a fair bit of noise in our program. Most of its lines of code are dealing with creating and managing a thread pool, which, while necessary, isn't central to the problem we're solving—it's an implementation detail.

We'll keep things as they are for the moment and add a new requirement: rolling averages.

Rolling averages

Now that we can see the up-to-date stock price for a given company, it makes sense to display a rolling average of the past, say, five stock prices. In a real scenario, this would provide an objective view of a company's share trend in the stock market.

Let's extend our program to accommodate this new requirement.

First, we'll need to modify our namespace definition:

```
(ns stock-market-monitor.core
  (:require [seesaw.core :refer :all])
  (:import (java.util.concurrent ScheduledThreadPoolExecutor
                                 TimeUnit)
           (clojure.lang PersistentQueue)))
```

The only change is a new import clause, for Clojure's `PersistentQueue` class. We will be using that later.

We'll also need a new label to display the current running average:

```
(def running-avg-label (label "Running average: -"))
(config! main-frame :content
         (border-panel
          :north  price-label
          :center running-avg-label
          :border 5))
```

Next, we need a function to calculate rolling averages. A rolling — or moving — average is a calculation in statistics, where you take the average of a subset of items in a dataset. This subset has a fixed size and it shifts forward as data comes in. This will become clear with an example.

Suppose you have a list with numbers from 1 to 10, inclusive. If we use 3 as the subset size, the rolling averages are as follows:

```
[1 2 3 4 5 6 7 8 9 10] => 2.0
[1 2 3 4 5 6 7 8 9 10] => 3.0
[1 2 3 4 5 6 7 8 9 10] => 4.0
```

The highlighted parts in the preceding code show the current *window* being used to calculate the subset average.

Now that we know what rolling averages are, we can move on to implement it in our program:

```
(defn roll-buffer [buffer num buffer-size]
  (let [buffer (conj buffer num)]
    (if (> (count buffer) buffer-size)
      (pop buffer)
      buffer)))

(defn avg [numbers]
  (float (/ (reduce + numbers)
            (count numbers))))

(defn make-running-avg [buffer-size]
  (let [buffer (atom clojure.lang.PersistentQueue/EMPTY)]
    (fn [n]
      (swap! buffer roll-buffer n buffer-size)
      (avg @buffer))))

(def running-avg (running-avg 5))
```

The `roll-buffer` function is a utility function that takes a queue, a number, and a buffer size as arguments. It adds that number to the queue, popping the oldest element if the queue goes over the buffer limit, thus causing its contents to *roll* over.

Next, we have a function for calculating the average of a collection of numbers. We cast the result to float if there's an uneven division.

Finally, the higher-order `make-running-avg` function returns a stateful, single argument function that closes over an empty persistent queue. This queue is used to keep track of the current subset of data.

We then create an instance of this function by calling it with a buffer size of 5 and save it to the `running-avg` var. Each time we call this new function with a number, it will add it to the queue using the `roll-buffer` function and then finally return the average of the items in the queue.

The code we have written to manage the thread pool will be reused as is so all that is left to do is update our periodic function:

```
(defn worker []
  (let [price (share-price "XYZ")]
    (->> (str "Price: " price) (text! price-label))
    (->> (str "Running average: " (running-avg price))
         (text! running-avg-label))))
```

```
(defn -main [& args]
  (show! main-frame)
  (.addShutdownHook (Runtime/getRuntime)
                    (Thread. #(shutdown @pool)))
  (init-scheduler 1)
  (run-every @pool 500
             #(invoke-now (worker)))))
```

Since our function isn't a one-liner anymore, we abstract it away in its own function called `worker`. As before, it updates the price label, but we have also extended it to use the `running-avg` function created earlier.

We're ready to run the program once more:

```
lein trampoline run -m stock-market-monitor.core
```

You should see a window like the one shown in the following screenshot:

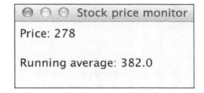

You should see that in addition to displaying the current share price for XYZ, the program also keeps track and refreshes the running average of the stream of prices.

Identifying problems with our current approach

Aside from the lines of code responsible for building the user interface, our program is roughly 48 lines long.

The core of the program resides in the `share-price` and `avg` functions, which are responsible for querying the price service and calculating the average of a list of n numbers, respectively. They represent only six lines of code. There is a lot of *incidental complexity* in this small program.

Incidental complexity is complexity caused by code that is not essential to the problem at hand. In this example, we have two sources of such complexity — we are disregarding UI specific code for this discussion: the thread pool and the rolling buffer function. They add a great deal of cognitive load to someone reading and maintaining the code.

The thread pool is external to our problem. It is only concerned with the semantics of how to run tasks asynchronously. The rolling buffer function specifies a detailed implementation of a queue and how to use it to represent the concept.

Ideally, we should be able to abstract over these details and focus on the core of our problem; **Compositional Event Systems** (CES) allows us to do just that.

Removing incidental complexity with RxClojure

In *Chapter 2, A Look at Reactive Extensions*, we learned about the basic building blocks of RxClojure, an open-source CES framework. In this section, we'll use this knowledge in order to remove the incidental complexity from our program. This will give us a clear, declarative way to display both prices and rolling averages.

The UI code we've written so far remains unchanged, but we need to make sure RxClojure is declared in the dependencies section of our `project.clj` file:

```
[io.reactivex/rxclojure "1.0.0"]
```

Then, ensure we require the following library:

```
(ns stock-market-monitor.core
  (:require [rx.lang.clojure.core :as rx]
            [seesaw.core :refer :all])
  (:import (java.util.concurrent TimeUnit)
           (rx Observable)))
```

The way we approach the problem this time is also different. Let's take a look at the first requirement: it requires we display the current price of a company's share in the stock market.

Every time we query the price service, we get a — possibly different — price for the company in question. As we saw in *Chapter 2, A Look at Reactive Extensions*, modeling this as an observable sequence is easy, so we'll start with that. We'll create a function that gives us back a stock price observable for the given company:

```
(defn make-price-obs [company-code]
  (rx/return (share-price company-code)))
```

This is an observable that yields a single value and terminates. It's equivalent to the following marble diagram:

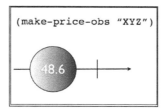

Part of the first requirement is that we query the service on a predefined time interval—every 500 milliseconds in this case. This hints at an observable we have encountered before, aptly named *interval*. In order to get the polling behavior we want, we need to combine the interval and the price observables.

As you probably recall, `flatmap` is the tool for the job here:

```
(rx/flatmap (fn [_] (make-price-obs "XYZ"))
            (Observable/interval 500
                                 TimeUnit/MILLISECONDS))
```

The preceding snippet creates an observable that will yield the latest stock price for XYZ every 500 milliseconds indefinitely. It corresponds to the following diagram:

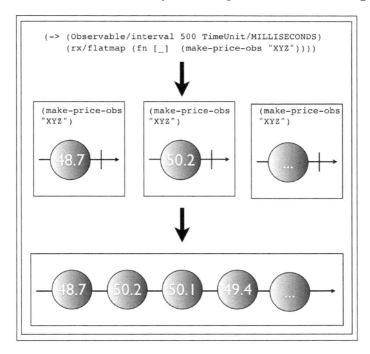

In fact, we can simply subscribe to this new observable and test it out. Modify your main function to the following snippet and run the program:

```
(defn -main [& args]
  (show! main-frame)
  (let [price-obs (rx/flatmap (fn [_] (make-price-obs "XYZ"))
                             (Observable/interval 500 TimeUnit/
MILLISECONDS))]
    (rx/subscribe price-obs
                  (fn [price]
                    (text! price-label (str "Price: " price)))))))
```

This is very cool! We replicated the behavior of our first program with only a few lines of code. The best part is that we did not have to worry about thread pools or scheduling actions. By thinking about the problem in terms of observable sequences, as well as combining existing and new observables, we were able to declaratively express what we want the program to do.

This already provides great benefits in maintainability and readability. However, we are still missing the other half of our program: rolling averages.

Observable rolling averages

It might not be immediately obvious how we can model rolling averages as observables. What we need to keep in mind is that pretty much anything we can think of as a sequence of values, we can probably model as an observable sequence.

Rolling averages are no different. Let's forget for a moment that the prices are coming from a network call wrapped in an observable. Let's imagine we have all values we care about in a Clojure vector:

```
(def values (range 10))
```

What we need is a way to process these values in partitions — or buffers — of size 5 in such a way that only a single value is dropped at each interaction. In Clojure, we can use the partition function for this purpose:

```
(doseq [buffer (partition 5 1 values)]
  (prn buffer))

(0 1 2 3 4)
(1 2 3 4 5)
(2 3 4 5 6)
(3 4 5 6 7)
(4 5 6 7 8)
...
```

The second argument to the `partition` function is called a *step* and it is the offset of how many items should be skipped before starting a new partition. Here, we set it to 1 in order to create the sliding window effect we need.

The big question then is: can we somehow leverage `partition` when working with observable sequences?

It turns out that RxJava has a transformer called `buffer` just for this purpose. The previous example can be rewritten as follows:

```
(-> (rx/seq->o (vec (range 10)))
    (.buffer 5 1)
    (rx/subscribe
     (fn [price]
        (prn (str "Value: " price)))))
```

> As mentioned previously, not all RxJava's API is exposed through RxClojure, so here we need to use interop to access the `buffer` method from the observable sequence.

As before, the second argument to `buffer` is the offset, but it's called `skip` in the RxJava documentation. If you run this at the REPL you'll see the following output:

```
"Value: [0, 1, 2, 3, 4]"
"Value: [1, 2, 3, 4, 5]"
"Value: [2, 3, 4, 5, 6]"
"Value: [3, 4, 5, 6, 7]"
"Value: [4, 5, 6, 7, 8]"
...
```

This is exactly what we want. The only difference is that the buffer method waits until it has enough elements—five in this case—before proceeding.

Now, we can go back to our program and incorporate this idea with our main function. Here is what it looks like:

```
(defn -main [& args]
  (show! main-frame)
  (let [price-obs (-> (rx/flatmap make-price-obs
                                  (Observable/interval 500 TimeUnit/
MILLISECONDS))
                      (.publish))
        sliding-buffer-obs (.buffer price-obs 5 1)]
    (rx/subscribe price-obs
                  (fn [price]
                    (text! price-label (str "Price: " price))))
```

```
(rx/subscribe sliding-buffer-obs
              (fn [buffer]
                  (text! running-avg-label (str "Running average: "
(avg buffer)))))))
    (.connect price-obs)))
```

The preceding snippet works by creating two observables. The first one, `price-obs`, we had created before. The new sliding buffer observable is created using the `buffer` transformer on `price-obs`.

We can, then, independently subscribe to each one in order to update the price and rolling average labels. Running the program will display the same screen we've seen previously:

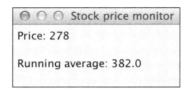

You might have noticed two method calls we hadn't seen before: `publish` and `connect`.

The `publish` method returns a connectable observable. This means that the observable won't start emitting values until its `connect` method has been called. We do this here because we want to make sure that all the subscribers receive all the values emitted by the original observable.

In conclusion, without much additional code, we implemented all requirements in a concise, declarative manner that is easy to maintain and follow. We have also made the previous roll-buffer function completely unnecessary.

The full source code for the CES version of the program is given here for reference:

```
(ns stock-market-monitor.05frp-price-monitor-rolling-avg
  (:require [rx.lang.clojure.core :as rx]
            [seesaw.core :refer :all])
  (:import (java.util.concurrent TimeUnit)
           (rx Observable)))

(native!)

(def main-frame (frame :title "Stock price monitor"
                       :width 200 :height 100
```

```
                              :on-close :exit))

(def price-label        (label "Price: -"))
(def running-avg-label (label "Running average: -"))

(config! main-frame :content
         (border-panel
          :north  price-label
          :center running-avg-label
          :border 5))

(defn share-price [company-code]
  (Thread/sleep 200)
  (rand-int 1000))

(defn avg [numbers]
  (float (/ (reduce + numbers)
            (count numbers))))

(defn make-price-obs [_]
  (rx/return (share-price "XYZ")))

(defn -main [& args]
  (show! main-frame)
  (let [price-obs (-> (rx/flatmap make-price-obs
                                  (Observable/interval 500 TimeUnit/
MILLISECONDS))
                      (.publish))
        sliding-buffer-obs (.buffer price-obs 5 1)]
    (rx/subscribe price-obs
                  (fn [price]
                    (text! price-label (str "Price: " price))))
    (rx/subscribe sliding-buffer-obs
                  (fn [buffer]
                    (text! running-avg-label (str "Running average: "
(avg buffer)))))
    (.connect price-obs)))
```

Note how in this version of the program, we didn't have to use a shutdown hook. This is because RxClojure creates daemon threads, which are automatically terminated once the application exits.

Summary

In this chapter, we simulated a real-world application with our stock market program. We've written it in a somewhat traditional way using thread pools and a custom queue implementation. We then refactored it to a CES style using RxClojure's observable sequences.

The resulting program is shorter, simpler, and easier to read once you get familiar with the core concepts of RxClojure and RxJava.

In the next Chapter we will be introduced to core.async in preparation for implementing our own basic CES framework.

4

Introduction to core.async

Long gone are the days when programs were required to do only one thing at a time. Being able to perform several tasks concurrently is at the core of the vast majority of modern business applications. This is where asynchronous programming comes in.

Asynchronous programming — and, more generally, concurrency — is about doing more with your hardware resources than you previously could. It means fetching data from the network or a database connection without having to wait for the result. Or, perhaps, reading an Excel spreadsheet into memory while the user can still operate the graphical interface. In general, it improves a system's responsiveness.

In this chapter, we will look at how different platforms handle this style of programming. More specifically, we will:

- Be introduced to core.async's background and API
- Solidify our understanding of core.async by re-implementing the stock market application in terms of its abstractions
- Understand how core.async deals with error handling and backpressure
- Take a brief tour on transducers

Asynchronous programming and concurrency

Different platforms have different programming models. For instance, JavaScript applications are single-threaded and have an event loop. When making a network call, it is common to register a callback that will be invoked at a later stage, when that network call completes either successfully or with an error.

In contrast, when we're on the JVM, we can take full advantage of multithreading to achieve concurrency. It is simple to spawn new threads via one of the many concurrency primitives provided by Clojure, such as futures.

However, asynchronous programming becomes cumbersome. Clojure futures don't provide a native way for us to be notified of their completion at a later stage. In addition, retrieving values from a not-yet-completed future is a blocking operation. This can be seen clearly in the following snippet:

```
(defn do-something-important []
  (let [f (future (do (prn "Calculating...")
                      (Thread/sleep 10000)))]
    (prn "Perhaps the future has done its job?")
    (prn @f)
    (prn "You will only see this in about 10 seconds...")))

(do-something-important)
```

The second call to print dereferences the future, causing the main thread to block since it hasn't finished yet. This is why you only see the last print after the thread in which the future is running has finished. Callbacks can, of course, be simulated by spawning a separate thread to monitor the first one, but this solution is clunky at best.

An exception to the lack of callbacks is GUI programming in Clojure. Much like JavaScript, Clojure Swing applications also possess an event loop and can respond to user input and invoke listeners (callbacks) to handle them.

Another option is rewriting the previous example with a custom callback that is passed into the future:

```
(defn do-something-important [callback]
  (let [f (future (let [answer 42]
                    (Thread/sleep 10000)
                    (callback answer)))]
    (prn "Perhaps the future has done its job?")
    (prn "You should see this almost immediately and then in 10
secs...")
    f))

(do-something-important (fn [answer]
                          (prn "Future is done. Answer is " answer)))
```

This time the order of the outputs should make more sense. However, if we return the future from this function, we have no way to give it another callback. We have lost the ability to perform an action when the future ends and are back to having to dereference it, thus blocking the main thread again—exactly what we wanted to avoid.

Java 8 introduces a new class, `CompletableFuture`, that allows registering a callback to be invoked once the future completes. If that's an option for you, you can use interop to make Clojure leverage the new class.

As you might have realized, CES is closely related to asynchronous programming: the stock market application we built in the previous chapter is an example of such a program. The main—or UI—thread is never blocked by the Observables fetching data from the network. Additionally, we were also able to register callbacks when subscribing to them.

In many asynchronous applications, however, callbacks are not the best way to go. Heavy use of callbacks can lead to what is known as callback hell. Clojure provides a more powerful and elegant solution.

In the next few sections, we will explore `core.async`, a Clojure library for asynchronous programming, and how it relates to Reactive Programming.

core.async

If you've ever done any amount of JavaScript programming, you have probably experienced callback hell. If you haven't, the following code should give you a good idea:

```
http.get('api/users/find?name=' + name, function(user){
  http.get('api/orders?userId=' + user.id, function(orders){
    orders.forEach(function(order){
      container.append(order);
    });
  });
});
```

This style of programming can easily get out of hand—instead of writing more natural, sequential steps to achieving a task, that logic is instead scattered across multiple callbacks, increasing the developer's cognitive load.

In response to this issue, the JavaScript community released several promises libraries that are meant to solve the issue. We can think of promises as empty boxes we can pass into and return from our functions. At some point in the future, another process might put a value inside this box.

As an example, the preceding snippet can be written with promises like the following:

```
http.get('api/users/find?name=' + name)
  .then(function(user){
    return http.get('api/orders?userId=' + user.id);
  })
  .then(function(orders){
    orders.forEach(function(order){
      container.append(order);
    });
  });
```

The preceding snippet shows how using promises can flatten your callback pyramid, but they don't eliminate callbacks. The then function is a public function of the promises API. It is definitely a step in the right direction as the code is composable and easier to read.

As we tend to think in sequences of steps, however, we would like to write the following:

```
user   = http.get('api/users/find?name=' + name);
orders = http.get('api/orders?userId=' + user.id);
orders.forEach(function(order){
  container.append(order);
});
```

Even though the code looks synchronous, the behavior should be no different from the previous examples. This is exactly what core.async lets us do in both Clojure and ClojureScript.

Communicating sequential processes

The core.async library is built on an old idea. The foundation upon which it lies was first described by Tony Hoare—of Quicksort fame—in his 1978 paper *Communicating Sequential Processes* (*CSP*; see http://www.cs.ucf.edu/courses/cop4020/sum2009/CSP-hoare.pdf). CSP has since been extended and implemented in several languages, the latest of which being Google's **Go** programming language.

It is beyond the scope of this book to go into the details of this seminal paper, so what follows is a simplified description of the main ideas.

In CSP, work is modeled using two main abstractions: channels and processes. CSP is also message-driven and, as such, it completely decouples the producer from the consumer of the message. It is useful to think of channels as blocking queues.

A simplistic approach demonstrating these basic abstractions is as follows:

```
(import 'java.util.concurrent.ArrayBlockingQueue)

(defn producer [c]
  (prn "Taking a nap")
  (Thread/sleep 5000)
  (prn "Now putting a name in queue...")
  (.put c "Leo"))

(defn consumer [c]
  (prn "Attempting to take value from queue now...")
  (prn (str "Got it. Hello " (.take c) "!")))

(def chan (ArrayBlockingQueue. 10))

(future (consumer chan))
(future (producer chan))
```

Running this code in the REPL should show us output similar to the following:

```
"Attempting to take value from queue now..."
"Taking a nap"
;; then 5 seconds later
"Now putting a name in que queue..."
"Got it. Hello Leo!"
```

In order not to block our program, we start both the consumer and the producer in their own threads using a future. Since the consumer was started first, we most likely will see its output immediately. However, as soon as it attempts to take a value from the channel—or queue—it will block. It will wait for a value to become available and will only proceed after the producer is done taking its nap—clearly a very important task.

Now, let's compare it with a solution using core.async. First, create a new leiningen project and add a dependency on it:

```
[org.clojure/core.async "0.1.278.0-76b25b-alpha"]
```

Now, type this in the REPL or in your core namespace:

```
(ns core-async-playground.core
  (:require [clojure.core.async :refer [go chan <! >! timeout]]))

(defn prn-with-thread-id [s]
  (prn (str s " - Thread id: " (.getId (Thread/currentThread)))))

(defn producer [c]
  (go (prn-with-thread-id "Taking a nap ")
      (<! (timeout 5000))
      (prn-with-thread-id "Now putting a name in que queue...")
      (>! c "Leo")))

(defn consumer [c]
  (go (prn-with-thread-id "Attempting to take value from queue now...")
      (prn-with-thread-id (str "Got it. Hello " (<! c) "!"))))

(def c (chan))

(consumer c)
(producer c)
```

This time we are using a helper function, `prn-with-thread-id`, which appends the current thread ID to the output string. I will explain why shortly, but apart from that, the output will have been equivalent to the previous one:

```
"Attempting to take value from queue now... - Thread id: 43"
"Taking a nap  - Thread id: 44"
"Now putting a name in que queue... - Thread id: 48"
"Got it. Hello Leo! - Thread id: 48"
```

Structurally, both solutions look fairly similar, but since we are using quite a few new functions here, let's break it down:

- `chan` is a function that creates a `core.async` channel. As mentioned previously, it can be thought of as a concurrent blocking queue and is the main abstraction in the library. By default `chan` creates an unbounded channel, but `core.async` provides many more useful channel constructors, a few of which we'll be using later.

- `timeout` is another such channel constructor. It gives us a *channel* that will *wait* for a given amount of time before returning nil to the taking process, closing itself immediately afterward. This is the `core.async` equivalent of **Thread/sleep**.

- The functions >! and <! are used to put and take values from a channel, respectively. The caveat is that they have to be used inside a go block, as we will explain later.

- go is a macro that takes a body of expressions — which form a go block — and creates lightweight processes. This is where the magic happens. Inside a go block, any calls to >! and <! that would ordinarily block waiting for values to be available in channels are instead parked. Parking is a special type of blocking used internally in the state machine of core.async. The blog post by Huey Petersen covers this state machine in depth (see http://hueypetersen.com/posts/2013/08/02/the-state-machines-of-core-async/).

Go blocks are the very reason for which I chose to print the thread IDs in our example. If we look closely, we'll realize that the last two statements were executed in the same thread — this isn't true 100 percent of the time as concurrency is inherently non-deterministic. This is a fundamental difference between core.async and solutions using threads/futures.

Threads can be expensive. On the JVM, their default stack size is 512 kilobytes — configurable via the -Xss JVM startup option. When developing a highly concurrent system, creating thousands of threads can quickly drain the resources of the machine the application is running on.

core.async acknowledges this limitation and gives us lightweight processes. Internally, they do share a thread pool, but instead of wastefully creating a thread per go block, threads are recycled and reused when a put/take operation is waiting for a value to become available.

 At the time of writing, the thread pool used by core.async defaults to the number of available processors x 2, + 42. So, a machine with eight processors will have a pool with 58 threads.

Therefore, it is common for core.async applications to have dozens of thousands of lightweight processes. They are extremely cheap to create.

Since this is a book on Reactive Programming, the question that might be in your head now is: can we build reactive applications using core.async? The short answer is yes, we can! To prove it, we will revisit our stock market application and rewrite it using core.async.

Rewriting the stock market application with core.async

By using an example we are familiar with, we are able to focus on the differences between all approaches discussed so far, without getting side tracked with new, specific domain rules.

Before we dive into the implementation, let's quickly do an overview of how our solution should work.

Just like in our previous implementations, we have a service from which we can query share prices. Where our approach differs, however, is a direct consequence of how `core.async` channels work.

On a given schedule, we would like to write the current price to a `core.async` channel. This might look like so:

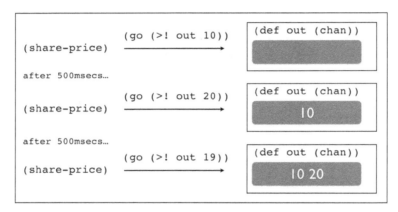

This process will continuously put prices in the `out` channel. We need to do two things with each price: display it and display the calculated sliding window. Since we like our functions decoupled, we will use two `go` blocks, one for each task:

Hold on. There seems to be something off with our approach. Once we take a price from the output channel, it is not available any longer to be taken by other go blocks, so, instead of calculating the sliding window starting with 10, our function ends up getting the second value, 20. With this approach, we will end up with a sliding window that calculates a sliding window with roughly every other item, depending on how consistent the interleaving between the go blocks is.

Clearly, this is not what we want, but it helps us think about the problem a little more. The semantics of core.async prevent us from reading a value from a channel more than once. Most of the time, this behavior is just fine—especially if you think of them as queues. So how can we provide the same value to both functions?

To solve this problem, we will take advantage of another channel constructor provided by core.async called broadcast. As the name implies, broadcast returns a channel, which, when written to, writes its value into the channels passed to it as arguments. Effectively, this changes our high-level picture to something like the following:

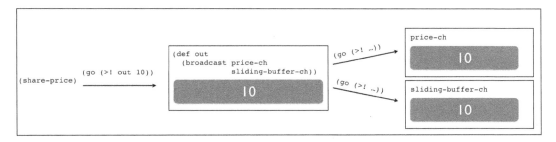

In summary, we will have a go loop writing prices to this broadcast channel, which will then forward its values to the two channels from which we will be operating: prices and the sliding window.

With the general idea in place, we are ready to dive into the code.

Implementing the application code

We already have a project depending on core.async that we created in the previous section, so we'll be working off that. Let's start by adding an extra dependency on seesaw to your project.clj file:

```
:dependencies [[org.clojure/clojure "1.5.1"]
               [org.clojure/core.async "0.1.278.0-76b25b-alpha"]
               [seesaw "1.4.4"]]
```

Next, create a file called `stock_market.clj` in the `src` directory and add this namespace declaration:

```
(ns core-async-playground.stock-market
  (:require [clojure.core.async
              :refer [go chan <! >! timeout go-loop map>] :as async])
  (:require [clojure.core.async.lab :refer [broadcast]])
  (:use [seesaw.core]))
```

This might be a good point to restart your REPL if you haven't done so. Don't worry about any functions we haven't seen yet. We'll get a feel for them in this section.

The GUI code remains largely unchanged, so no explanation should be necessary for the next snippet:

```
(native!)

(def main-frame (frame :title "Stock price monitor"
                       :width 200 :height 100
                       :on-close :exit))

(def price-label      (label "Price: -"))
(def running-avg-label (label "Running average: -"))

(config! main-frame :content
         (border-panel
          :north  price-label
          :center running-avg-label
          :border 5))

(defn share-price [company-code]
  (Thread/sleep 200)
  (rand-int 1000))

(defn avg [numbers]
  (float (/ (reduce + numbers)
            (count numbers))))

(defn roll-buffer [buffer val buffer-size]
  (let [buffer (conj buffer val)]
    (if (> (count buffer) buffer-size)
      (pop buffer)
      buffer)))
```

```
(defn make-sliding-buffer [buffer-size]
  (let [buffer (atom clojure.lang.PersistentQueue/EMPTY)]
    (fn [n]
      (swap! buffer roll-buffer n buffer-size)))))

(def sliding-buffer (make-sliding-buffer 5))
```

The only difference is that now we have a `sliding-buffer` function that returns a window of data. This is in contrast with our original application, where the `rolling-avg` function was responsible for both creating the window and calculating the average. This new design is more general as it makes this function easier to reuse. The sliding logic is the same, however.

Next, we have our main application logic using `core.async`:

```
(defn broadcast-at-interval [msecs task & ports]
  (go-loop [out (apply broadcast ports)]
    (<! (timeout msecs))
    (>! out (task))
    (recur out)))

(defn -main [& args]
  (show! main-frame)
  (let [prices-ch          (chan)
        sliding-buffer-ch  (map> sliding-buffer (chan))]
    (broadcast-at-interval 500 #(share-price "XYZ") prices-ch sliding-
buffer-ch)
    (go-loop []
      (when-let [price (<! prices-ch)]
        (text! price-label (str "Price: " price))
        (recur)))
    (go-loop []
      (when-let [buffer (<! sliding-buffer-ch)]
        (text! running-avg-label (str "Running average: " (avg
buffer)))
        (recur)))))
```

Let's walk through the code.

The first function, `broadcast-at-interval`, is responsible for creating the broadcasting channel. It receives a variable number of arguments: a number of milliseconds describing the interval, the function representing the task to be executed, and a sequence of one of more output channels. These channels are used to create the broadcasting channel to which the go loop will be writing prices.

Next, we have our main function. The `let` block is where the interesting bits are. As we discussed in our high-level diagrams, we need two output channels: one for prices and one for the sliding window. They are both created in the following:

```
. . .
(let [prices-ch         (chan)
      sliding-buffer-ch (map> sliding-buffer (chan))]
. . .
```

`prices-ch` should be self-explanatory; however, `sliding-buffer-ch` is using a function we haven't encountered before: `map>`. This is yet another useful channel constructor in `core.async`. It takes two arguments: a function and a target channel. It returns a channel that applies this function to each value before writing it to the target channel. An example will help illustrate how it works:

```
(def c (map> sliding-buffer (chan 10)))
(go (doseq [n (range 10)]
      (>! c n)))
(go (doseq [n (range 10)]
      (prn (vec (<! c)))))

;; [0]
;; [0 1]
;; [0 1 2]
;; [0 1 2 3]
;; [0 1 2 3 4]
;; [1 2 3 4 5]
;; [2 3 4 5 6]
;; [3 4 5 6 7]
;; [4 5 6 7 8]
;; [5 6 7 8 9]
```

That is, we write a price to the channel and get a sliding window on the other end. Finally, we create the two go blocks containing the side effects. They loop indefinitely, getting values from both channels and updating the user interface.

You can see it in action by running the program from the terminal:

```
$ lein run -m core-async-playground.stock-market
```

Error handling

Back in *Chapter 2, A Look at Reactive Extensions*, we learned how Reactive Extensions treats errors and exceptions. It provides a rich set of combinators to deal with exceptional cases and are straightforward to use.

Despite being a pleasure to work with, `core.async` doesn't ship with much support for exception handling. In fact, if we write our code with only the happy path in mind we don't even know an error occurred!

Let's have a look at an example:

```
(defn get-data []
  (throw (Exception. "Bad things happen!")))

(defn process []
  (let [result (chan)]
    ;; do some processing...
    (go (>! result (get-data)))
    result))
```

In the preceding snippet, we introduced two functions:

- `get-data` simulates a function that fetches data from the network or an in-memory cache. In this case it simply throws an exception.
- `process` is a function that depends on `get-data` to do something interesting and puts the result into a channel, which is returned at the end.

Let's watch what happens when we put this together:

```
(go (let [result (<! (->> (process "data")
                          (map> #(* % %))
                          (map> #(prn %))))]
      (prn "result is: " result)))
```

Nothing happens. Zero, zip, zilch, nada.

This is precisely the problem with error handling in `core.async`: by default, our exceptions are swallowed by the go block as it runs on a separate thread. We are left in this state where we don't really know what happened.

Not all is lost, however. David Nolen outlined on his blog a pattern for dealing with such asynchronous exceptions. It only requires a few extra lines of code.

We start by defining a helper function and macro—this would probably live in a utility namespace we require anywhere we use `core.async`:

```
(defn throw-err [e]
  (when (instance? Throwable e) (throw e))
  e)

(defmacro <? [ch]
  `(throw-err (async/<! ~ch)))
```

The `throw-err` function receives a value and, if it's a subclass of `Throwable`, it is thrown. Otherwise, it is simply returned.

The macro `<?` is essentially a drop-in replacement for `<!`. In fact, it uses `<!` to get the value out of the channel but passes it to `throw-err` first.

With these utilities in place, we need to make a couple of changes, first to our `process` function:

```
(defn process []
  (let [result (chan)]
    ;; do some processing...
    (go (>! result (try (get-data)
                        (catch Exception e
                          e))))
    result))
```

The only change is that we wrapped `get-data` in a `try`/`catch` block. Look closely at the `catch` block: it simply returns the exception.

This is important as we need to ensure the exception gets put into the channel.

Next, we update our consumer code:

```
(go (try (let [result  (<? (->> (process "data")
                                (map> #(* % %))
                                (map> #(prn %))))]
           (prn "result is: " result))
         (catch Exception e
           (prn "Oops, an error happened! We better do something about it
here!"))))
;; "Oops, an error happened! We better do something about it here!"
```

This time we use `<?` in place of `<!`. This makes sense as it will rethrow any exceptions found in the channel. As a result we can now use a simple `try`/`catch` to regain control over our exceptions.

Backpressure

The main mechanism by which `core.async` allows for coordinating backpressure is buffering. `core.async` doesn't allow unbounded buffers as this can be a source of bugs and a resource hog.

Instead, we are required to think hard about our application's unique needs and choose an appropriate buffering strategy.

Fixed buffer

This is the simplest form of buffering. It is fixed to a chosen number n, allowing producers to put items in the channel without having to wait for consumers:

```
(def result (chan (buffer 5)))
(go-loop []
  (<! (async/timeout 1000))
  (when-let [x (<! result)]
    (prn "Got value: " x)
    (recur)))

(go  (doseq [n (range 5)]
       (>! result n))
     (prn "Done putting values!")
     (close! result))

;; "Done putting values!"
;; "Got value: " 0
;; "Got value: " 1
;; "Got value: " 2
;; "Got value: " 3
;; "Got value: " 4
```

In the preceding example, we created a buffer of size 5 and started a go loop to consume values from it. The go loop uses a timeout channel to delay its start.

Then, we start another go block that puts numbers from 0 to 4 into the result channel and prints to the console once it's done.

By then, the first timeout will have expired and we will see the values printed to the REPL.

Now let's watch what happens if the buffer isn't large enough:

```
(def result (chan (buffer 2)))
(go-loop []
  (<! (async/timeout 1000))
  (when-let [x (<! result)]
    (prn "Got value: " x)
    (recur)))

(go  (doseq [n (range 5)]
       (>! result n))
     (prn "Done putting values!")
     (close! Result))
```

```
;; "Got value: " 0
;; "Got value: " 1
;; "Got value: " 2
;; "Done putting values!"
;; "Got value: " 3
;; "Got value: " 4
```

This time our buffer size is 2 but everything else is the same. As you can see the go loop finishes much later as it attempted to put another value in the result channel and was blocked/parked since its buffer was full.

As with most things, this might be OK but if we are not willing to block a fast producer just because we can't consume its items fast enough, we must look for another option.

Dropping buffer

A dropping buffer also has a fixed size. However, instead of blocking producers when it is full, it simply ignores any new items as shown here:

```
(def result (chan (dropping-buffer 2)))
(go-loop []
  (<! (async/timeout 1000))
  (when-let [x (<! result)]
    (prn "Got value: " x)
    (recur)))

(go (doseq [n (range 5)]
      (>! result n))
    (prn "Done putting values!")
    (close! result))

;; "Done putting values!"
;; "Got value: " 0
;; "Got value: " 1
```

As before, we still have a buffer of size two, but this time the producer ends quickly without ever getting blocked. The dropping-buffer simply ignored all items over its limit.

Sliding buffer

A drawback of dropping buffers is that we might not be processing the latest items at a given time. For the times where processing the latest information is a must, we can use a sliding buffer:

```
(def result (chan (sliding-buffer 2)))
(go-loop []
  (<! (async/timeout 1000))
  (when-let [x (<! result)]
    (prn "Got value: " x)
    (recur)))

(go  (doseq [n (range 5)]
       (>! result n))
     (prn "Done putting values!")
     (close! result))

;; "Done putting values!"
;; "Got value: " 3
;; "Got value: " 4
```

As before, we only get two values but they are the latest ones produced by the go loop.

When the limit of the sliding buffer is overrun, core.async drops the oldest items to make room for the newest ones. I end up using this buffering strategy most of the time.

Transducers

Before we finish up with our core.async portion of the book, it would be unwise of me not to mention what is coming up in Clojure 1.7 as well as how this affects core.async.

At the time of this writing, Clojure's latest release is 1.7.0-alpha5 — and even though it is an alpha release, a lot of people — myself included — are already using it in production.

As such, a final version could be just around the corner and perhaps by the time you read this, 1.7 final will be out already.

One of the big changes in this upcoming release is the introduction of transducers. We will not cover the nuts and bolts of it here but rather focus on what it means at a high-level with examples using both Clojure sequences and core.async channels.

If you would like to know more I recommend Carin Meier's *Green Eggs and Transducers* blog post (`http://gigasquidsoftware.com/blog/2014/09/06/green-eggs-and-transducers/`). It's a great place to start.

Additionally, the official Clojure documentation site on the subject is another useful resource (`http://clojure.org/transducers`).

Let's get started by creating a new leiningen project:

```
$ lein new core-async-transducers
```

Now, open your `project.clj` file and make sure you have the right dependencies:

```
    . . .
    :dependencies [[org.clojure/clojure "1.7.0-alpha5"]
                   [org.clojure/core.async "0.1.346.0-17112a-alpha"]]
    . . .
```

Next, fire up a REPL session in the project root and require `core.async`, which we will be using shortly:

```
$ lein repl
user> (require '[clojure.core.async :refer [go chan map< filter< into >!
<! go-loop close! pipe]])
```

We will start with a familiar example:

```
(->> (range 10)
     (map inc)           ;; creates a new sequence
     (filter even?)      ;; creates a new sequence
     (prn "result is "))
;; "result is " (2 4 6 8 10)
```

The preceding snippet is straightforward and highlights an interesting property of what happens when we apply combinators to Clojure sequences: each combinator creates an intermediate sequence.

In the previous example, we ended up with three in total: the one created by `range`, the one created by `map`, and finally the one created by `filter`. Most of the time, this won't really be an issue but for large sequences this means a lot of unnecessary allocation.

Starting in Clojure 1.7, the previous example can be written like so:

```
(def xform
  (comp (map inc)
        (filter even?)))   ;; no intermediate sequence created
```

```
(->> (range 10)
     (sequence xform)
     (prn "result is "))
;; "result is " (2 4 6 8 10)
```

The Clojure documentation describes transducers as composable algorithmic transformations. Let's see why that is.

In the new version, a whole range of the core sequence combinators, such as `map` and `filter`, have gained an extra arity: if you don't pass it a collection, it instead returns a transducer.

In the previous example, `(map inc)` returns a transducer that knows how to apply the function `inc` to elements of a sequence. Similarly, `(filter even?)` returns a transducer that will eventually filter elements of a sequence. Neither of them do anything yet, they simply return functions.

This is interesting because transducers are composable. We build larger and more complex transducers by using simple function composition:

```
(def xform
  (comp (map inc)
        (filter even?))))
```

Once we have our transducer ready, we can apply it to a collection in a few different ways. For this example, we chose `sequence` as it will return a lazy sequence of the applications of the given transducer to the input sequence:

```
(->> (range 10)
     (sequence xform)
     (prn "result is "))
;; "result is " (2 4 6 8 10)
```

As previously highlighted, this code does not create intermediate sequences; transducers extract the very core of the algorithmic transformation at hand and abstracts it away from having to deal with sequences directly.

Transducers and core.async

We might now be asking ourselves "What do transducers have to do with `core.async?`"

It turns out that once we're able to extract the core of these transformations and put them together using simple function composition, there is nothing stopping us from using transducers with data structures other than sequences!

Let's revisit our first example using standard `core.async` functions:

```
(def result (chan 10))

(def transformed
  (->> result
       (map< inc)         ;; creates a new channel
       (filter< even?) ;; creates a new channel
       (into []))))


(go
  (prn "result is " (<! transformed)))

(go
  (doseq [n (range 10)]
    (>! result n))
  (close! result))

;; "result is " [2 4 6 8 10]
```

This code should look familiar by now: it's the `core.async` equivalent of the sequence-only version shown earlier. As before, we have unnecessary allocations here as well, except that this time we're allocating channels.

With the new support for transducers, `core.async` can take advantage of the same transformation defined earlier:

```
(def result (chan 10))

(def xform
     (comp (map inc)
           (filter even?)))   ;; no intermediate channels created

(def transformed (->> (pipe result (chan 10 xform))
                      (into []))))


(go
  (prn "result is " (<! transformed)))

(go
  (doseq [n (range 10)]
    (>! result n))
```

```
      (close! result))

  ;; "result is " [2 4 6 8 10]
```

The code remains largely unchanged except we now use the same `xform` transformation defined earlier when creating a new channel. It's important to note that we did not have to use `core.async` combinators—in fact a lot of these combinators have been deprecated and will be removed in future versions of `core.async`.

The functions `map` and `filter` used to define `xform` are the same ones we used previously, that is, they are core Clojure functions.

This is the next big advantage of using transducers: by removing the underlying data structure from the equation via transducers, libraries such as `core.async` can reuse Clojure's core combinators to prevent unnecessary allocation and code duplication.

It's not too far fetched to imagine other frameworks like RxClojure could take advantage of transducers as well. All of them would be able to use the same core function across substantially different data structures and contexts: sequences, channels, and Obervables.

The concept of extracting the essence of computations disregarding their underlying data structures is an exciting topic and has been seen before in the Haskell community, although they deal with lists specifically.

Two papers worth mentioning on the subject are *Stream Fusion* [11] by Duncan Coutts, Roman Leshchinskiy and Don Stewart and *Transforming programs to eliminate trees* [12] by Philip Wadler. There are some overlaps so the reader might find these interesting.

Summary

By now, I hope to have proved that you can write reactive applications using `core.async`. It's an extremely powerful and flexible concurrency model with a rich API. If you can design your solution in terms of queues, most likely `core.async` is the tool you want to reach for.

This version of the stock market application is shorter and simpler than the version using only the standard Java API we developed earlier in this book—for instance, we didn't have to worry about thread pools. On the other hand, it feels like it is a little more complex than the version implemented using Reactive Extensions in *Chapter 3, Asynchronous Programming and Networking*.

This is because core.async operates at a lower level of abstraction when compared to other frameworks. This becomes especially obvious in our application as we had to worry about creating broadcasting channels, go loops, and so on—all of which can be considered incidental complexity, not directly related to the problem at hand.

core.async does, however, provide an excellent foundation for building our own CES abstractions. This is what we will be exploring next.

5
Creating Your Own CES Framework with core.async

In the previous chapter, it was alluded to that `core.async` operates at a lower level of abstraction when compared to other frameworks such as RxClojure or RxJava.

This is because most of the time we have to think carefully about the channels we are creating as well as what types and sizes of buffers to use, whether we need pub/sub functionality, and so on.

Not all applications require such level of control, however. Now that we are familiar with the motivations and main abstractions of `core.async` we can embark into writing a minimal CES framework using `core.async` as the underlying foundation.

By doing so, we avoid having to think about thread pool management as the framework takes care of that for us.

In this chapter, we will cover the following topics:

- Building a CES framework using `core.async` as its underlying concurrency strategy
- Building an application that uses our CES framework
- Understanding the trade-offs of the different approaches presented so far

A minimal CES framework

Before we get start on the details, we should define at a high level what *minimal* means.

Let's start with the two main abstractions our framework will provide: behaviors and event streams.

If you can recall from *Chapter 1, What is Reactive Programming?*, behaviors represent continuous, time-varying values such as time or a mouse position behavior. Event streams, on the other hand, represent discrete occurrences at a point in time *T*, such as key press.

Next, we should think about what kinds of operations we would like to support. Behaviors are fairly simple so at the very minimum we need to:

- Create new behaviors
- Retrieve the current value of a behavior
- Convert a behavior into an event stream

Event streams have more interesting logic in play and we should at least support these operations:

- Push/deliver a value down the stream
- Create a stream from a given interval
- Transform the stream with the `map` and `filter` operations
- Combine streams with `flatmap`
- Subscribe to a stream

This is a small subset but big enough to demonstrate the overall architecture of a CES framework. Once we're done, we'll use it to build a simple example.

Clojure or ClojureScript?

Here we'll shift gears and add another requirement to our little library: it should work both in Clojure and ClojureScript. At first, this might sound like a tough requirement. However, remember that `core.async` — the foundation of our framework — works both on the JVM and in JavaScript. This means we have a lot less work to do to make it happen.

It does mean, however, that we need to be capable of producing two artifacts from our library: a `jar` file and a JavaScript file. Luckily, there are leiningen plugins, which help us do that and we will be using a couple of them:

- `lein-cljsbuild` (see `https://github.com/emezeske/lein-cljsbuild`): Leiningen plugin to make building ClojureScript easy
- `cljx` (see `https://github.com/lynaghk/cljx`): A preprocessor used to write portable Clojure codebases, that is, write a single file and output both `.clj` and `.cljs` files

You don't need to understand these libraries in great detail. We are only using their basic functionality and will be explaining the bits and pieces as we encounter them.

Let's get started by creating a new leiningen project. We'll call our framework respondent—one of the many synonyms for the word reactive:

```
$ lein new respondent
```

We need to make a few changes to the project.clj file to include the dependencies and configurations we'll be using. First, make sure the project dependencies look like the following:

```
:dependencies [[org.clojure/clojure "1.5.1"]
               [org.clojure/core.async "0.1.303.0-886421-alpha"]
               [org.clojure/clojurescript "0.0-2202"]]
```

There should be no surprises here. Still in the project file, add the necessary plugins:

```
:plugins [[com.keminglabs/cljx "0.3.2"]
          [lein-cljsbuild "1.0.3"]]
```

These are the plugins that we've mentioned previously. By themselves they don't do much, however, and need to be configured.

For cljx, add the following to the project file:

```
:cljx {:builds [{:source-paths ["src/cljx"]
                 :output-path "target/classes"
                 :rules :clj}

                {:source-paths ["src/cljx"]
                 :output-path "target/classes"
                 :rules :cljs}]}
 :hooks [cljx.hooks]
```

The previous snippet deserves some explanation. cljx allows us to write code that is portable between Clojure and ClojureScript by placing annotations its preprocessor can understand. We will see later what these annotations look like, but this chunk of configuration tells cljx where to find the annotated files and where to output them once they're processed.

For example, based on the preceding rules, if we have a file called src/cljx/core.cljx and we run the preprocessor we will end up with the target/classes/core.clj and target/classes/core.cljs output files. The hooks, on the other hand, are simply a convenient way to automatically run cljx whenever we start a REPL session.

The next part of the configuration is for `cljsbuild`:

```
:cljsbuild
{:builds [{:source-paths ["target/classes"]
           :compiler {:output-to "target/main.js"}}]}
```

`cljsbuild` provides leiningen tasks to compile Cloduresript source code into JavaScript. We know from our preceding `cljx` configuration that the `source.cljs` files will be under `target/classes`, so here we're simply telling `cljsbuild` to compile all ClojureScript files in that directory and spit the contents to `target/main.js`. This is the last piece needed for the project file.

Go ahead and delete these files created by the leiningen template as we won't be using them:

```
$ rm src/respondent/core.clj
$ rm test/respondent/core_test.clj
```

Then, create a new `core.cljx` file under `src/cljx/respondent/` and add the following namespace declaration:

```
(ns respondent.core
  (:refer-clojure :exclude [filter map deliver])

  #+clj
  (:import [clojure.lang IDeref])

  #+clj
  (:require [clojure.core.async :as async
             :refer [go go-loop chan <! >! timeout
                     map> filter> close! mult tap untap]])
  #+cljs
  (:require [cljs.core.async :as async
             :refer [chan <! >! timeout map> filter>
                     close! mult tap untap]])

  #+cljs
  (:require-macros [respondent.core :refer [behavior]]
                   [cljs.core.async.macros :refer [go go-loop]]))
```

Here, we start seeing `cljx` annotations. `cljx` is simply a text preprocessor, so when it is processing a file using `clj` rules—as seen in the configuration—it will keep the s-expressions preceded by the annotation `#+clj` in the output file, while removing the ones prefixed by `#+cljs`. The reverse process happens when using `cljs` rules.

This is necessary because macros need to be compiled on the JVM, so they have to be included separately using the `:require-macros` namespace option when using ClojureScript. Don't worry about the `core.async` functions we haven't encountered before; they will be explained as we use them to build our framework.

Also, note how we are excluding functions from the Clojure standard API as we wish to use the same names and don't want any undesired naming collisions.

This section set us up with a new project and the plugins and configurations needed for our framework. We're ready to start implementing it.

Designing the public API

One of the requirements for behaviors we agreed on is the ability to turn a given behavior into an event stream. A common way of doing this is by sampling a behavior at a specific interval. If we take the *mouse position* behavior as an example, by sampling it every *x* seconds we get an event stream, which will emit the current mouse position at discrete points in time.

This leads to the following protocol:

```
(defprotocol IBehavior
  (sample [b interval]
    "Turns this Behavior into an EventStream from the sampled values
at the given interval"))
```

It has a single function, `sample`, which we described in the preceding code. There are more things we need to do with a behavior, but for now this will suffice.

Our next main abstraction is `EventStream`, which — based on the requirements seen previously — leads to the following protocol:

```
(defprotocol IEventStream
  (map       [s f]
    "Returns a new stream containing the result of applying f
    to the values in s")
  (filter    [s pred]
    "Returns a new stream containing the items from s
    for which pred returns true")
  (flatmap   [s f]
    "Takes a function f from values in s to a new EventStream.
    Returns an EventStream containing values from all underlying
streams combined.")
  (deliver   [s value]
    "Delivers a value to the stream s")
```

```
(completed? [s]
  "Returns true if this stream has stopped emitting values. False
otherwise."))
```

This gives us a few basic functions to transform and query an event stream. It does leave out the ability to subscribe to a stream. Don't worry, I didn't forget it!

Although, it is common to subscribe to an event stream, the protocol itself doesn't mandate it and this is because the operation fits best in its own protocol:

```
(defprotocol IObservable
  (subscribe [obs f] "Register a callback to be invoked when the
underlying source changes.
    Returns a token the subscriber can use to cancel the
subscription."))
```

As far as subscriptions go, it is useful to have a way of unsubscribing from a stream. This can be implemented in a couple of ways, but docstring of the preceding function hints at a specific one: a token that can be used to unsubscribe from a stream. This leads to our last protocol:

```
(defprotocol IToken
  (dispose [tk]
    "Called when the subscriber isn't interested in receiving more
items"))
```

Implementing tokens

The token type is the simplest in the whole framework as it has got a single function with a straightforward implementation:

```
(deftype Token [ch]
  IToken
  (dispose [_]
    (close! ch)))
```

It simply closes whatever channel it is given, stopping events from flowing through subscriptions.

Implementing event streams

The event stream implementation, on the other hand, is the most complex in our framework. We'll tackle it gradually, implementing and experimenting as we go.

First, let's look at our main constructor function, event-stream:

```
(defn event-stream
  "Creates and returns a new event stream. You can optionally provide
an existing
  core.async channel as the source for the new stream"
  ([]
     (event-stream (chan)))
  ([ch]
     (let [multiple  (mult ch)
           completed (atom false)]
       (EventStream. ch multiple completed))))
```

The docstring should be sufficient to understand the public API. What might not be clear, however, is what all the constructor arguments mean. From left to right, the arguments to EventStream are:

- ch: This is the core.async channel backing this stream.

- multiple: This is a way to broadcast information from one channel to many other channels. It's a core.async concept we will be explaining shortly.

- completed: A Boolean flag indicating whether this event stream has completed and will not emit any new values.

From the implementation, you can see that the multiple is created from the channel backing the stream. multiple works kind of like a broadcast. Consider the following example:

```
(def in (chan))
(def multiple (mult in))

(def out-1 (chan))
(tap multiple out-1)

(def out-2 (chan))
(tap multiple out-2)
(go (>! in "Single put!"))

(go (prn "Got from out-1 " (<! out-1)))
(go (prn "Got from out-2 " (<! out-2)))
```

In the previous snippet, we create an input channel, in, and mult of it called multiple. Then, we create two output channels, out-1 and out-2, which are both followed by a call to tap. This essentially means that whatever values are written to in will be taken by multiple and written to any channels tapped into it as the following output shows:

```
"Got from out-1 " "Single put!"
"Got from out-2 " "Single put!"
```

This will make understanding the EventStream implementation easier.

Next, let's have a look at what a minimal implementation of the EventStream looks like the following — make sure the implementation goes before the constructor function described earlier:

```
(declare event-stream)

(deftype EventStream [channel multiple completed]
  IEventStream
  (map [_ f]
    (let [out (map> f (chan))]
      (tap multiple out)
      (event-stream out)))

  (deliver [_ value]
    (if (= value ::complete)
      (do (reset! completed true)
          (go (>! channel value)
              (close! channel)))
      (go (>! channel value)))))


  IObservable
  (subscribe [this f]
    (let [out (chan)]
      (tap multiple out)
      (go-loop []
        (let [value (<! out)]
          (when (and value (not= value ::complete))
            (f value)
            (recur))))
      (Token. out))))
```

For now, we have chosen to implement only the map and deliver functions from the IEventStream protocol. This allows us to deliver values to the stream as well as transform those values.

However, this would not be very useful if we could not retrieve the values delivered. This is why we also implement the subscribe function from the IObservable protocol.

In a nutshell, map needs to take a value from the input stream, apply a function to it, and send it to the newly created stream. We do this by creating an output channel that taps on current multiple. We then use this channel to back the new event stream.

The deliver function simply puts the value into the backing channel. If the value is the namespaced keyword ::complete, we update the completed atom and close the backing channel. This ensures the stream will not emit any other values.

Finally, we have the subscribe function. The way subscribers are notified is by using an output channel tapped to backing multiple. We loop indefinitely calling the subscribing function whenever a new value is emitted.

We finish by returning a token, which will close the output channel once disposed, causing the go-loop to stop.

Let's make sure that all this makes sense by experimenting with a couple of examples in the REPL:

```
(def es1 (event-stream))
(subscribe es1 #(prn "first event stream emitted: " %))
(deliver es1 10)
;; "first event stream emitted: " 10


(def es2 (map es1 #(* 2 %)))
(subscribe es2 #(prn "second event stream emitted: " %))

(deliver es1 20)
;; "first event stream emitted: " 20
;; "second event stream emitted: " 40
```

Excellent! We have a minimal, working implementation of our IEventStream protocol!

The next function we'll implement is filter and it is very similar to map:

```
(filter [_ pred]
  (let [out (filter> pred (chan))]
    (tap multiple out)
    (event-stream out)))
```

The only difference is that we use the `filter>` function and `pred` should be a Boolean function:

```
(def es1 (event-stream))
(def es2 (filter es1 even?))
(subscribe es1 #(prn "first event stream emitted: " %))
(subscribe es2 #(prn "second event stream emitted: " %))

(deliver es1 2)
(deliver es1 3)
(deliver es1 4)

;; "first event stream emitted: " 2
;; "second event stream emitted: " 2
;; "first event stream emitted: " 3
;; "first event stream emitted: " 4
;; "second event stream emitted: " 4
```

As we witness, `es2` only emits a new value if and only if that value is an even number.

If you are following along, typing the examples step by step, you will need to restart your REPL whenever we add new functions to any `deftype` definition. This is because `deftype` generates and compiles a Java class when evaluated. As such, simply reloading the namespace won't be enough.

Alternatively, you can use a tool such as `tools.namespace` (see `https://github.com/clojure/tools.namespace`) that addresses some of these REPL reloading limitations.

Moving down our list, we now have `flatmap`:

```
(flatmap [_ f]
    (let [es (event-stream)
          out (chan)]
      (tap multiple out)
      (go-loop []
        (when-let [a (<! out)]
          (let [mb (f a)]
            (subscribe mb (fn [b]
                            (deliver es b)))
            (recur))))
      es))
```

We've encountered this operator before when surveying Reactive Extensions. This is what our docstring says about it:

Takes a function f from values in s to a new EventStream.

Returns an EventStream containing values from all underlying streams combined.

This means `flatmap` needs to combine all the possible event streams into a single output event stream. As before, we tap a new channel to the `multiple` stream, but then we loop over the output channel, applying `f` to each output value.

However, as we saw, `f` itself returns a new event stream, so we simply subscribe to it. Whenever the function registered in the subscription gets called, we deliver that value to the output event stream, effectively combining all streams into a single one.

Consider the following example:

```
(defn range-es [n]
  (let [es (event-stream (chan n))]
    (doseq [n (range n)]
      (deliver es n))
    es))

(def es1 (event-stream))
(def es2 (flatmap es1 range-es))
(subscribe es1 #(prn "first event stream emitted: " %))
(subscribe es2 #(prn "second event stream emitted: " %))

(deliver es1 2)
;; "first event stream emitted: " 2
;; "second event stream emitted: " 0
;; "second event stream emitted: " 1

(deliver es1 3)
;; "first event stream emitted: " 3
;; "second event stream emitted: " 0
;; "second event stream emitted: " 1
;; "second event stream emitted: " 2
```

We have a function, `range-es`, that receives a number n and returns an event stream that emits numbers from 0 to n. As before, we have a starting stream, es1, and a transformed stream created with `flatmap`, es2.

We can see from the preceding output that the stream created by `range-es` gets flattened into es2 allowing us to receive all values by simply subscribing to it once.

This leaves us with single function from IEventStream left to implement:

```
(completed? [_] @completed)
```

completed? simply returns the current value of the completed atom. We are now ready to implement behaviors.

Implementing behaviors

If you recall, the IBehavior protocol has a single function called sample whose docstring states: *Turns this Behavior into an EventStream from the sampled values at the given interval.*

In order to implement sample, we will first create a useful helper function that we will call from-interval:

```
(defn from-interval
  "Creates and returns a new event stream which emits values at the
given
interval.
  If no other arguments are given, the values start at 0 and increment
by
one at each delivery.

  If given seed and succ it emits seed and applies succ to seed to get
the next value. It then applies succ to the previous result and so
on."
  ([msecs]
    (from-interval msecs 0 inc))
  ([msecs seed succ]
    (let [es (event-stream)]
      (go-loop [timeout-ch (timeout msecs)
                value seed]
        (when-not (completed? es)
          (<! timeout-ch)
          (deliver es value)
          (recur (timeout msecs) (succ value))))
      es)))
```

The docstring function should be clear enough at this stage, but we would like to ensure we understand its behavior correctly by trying it at the REPL:

```
(def es1 (from-interval 500))
(def es1-token (subscribe es1 #(prn "Got: " %)))
;; "Got: " 0
```

```
;; "Got: " 1
;; "Got: " 2
;; "Got: " 3
;; ...
(dispose es1-token)
```

As expected, `es1` emits integers starting at zero at 500-millisecond intervals. By default, it would emit numbers indefinitely; therefore, we keep a reference to the token returned by calling `subscribe`.

This way we can dispose it whenever we're done, causing `es-1` to complete and stop emitting items.

Next, we can finally implement the `Behavior` type:

```
(deftype Behavior [f]
  IBehavior
  (sample [_ interval]
    (from-interval interval (f) (fn [& args] (f)))))
  IDeref
  (#+clj deref #+cljs -deref [_]
    (f)))

(defmacro behavior [& body]
  `(Behavior. #(do ~@body)))
```

A behavior is created by passing it a function. You can think of this function as a generator responsible for generating the next value in this event stream.

This generator function will be called whenever we (1) `deref` the `Behavior` or (2) at the interval given to `sample`.

The `behavior` macro is there for convenience and allows us to create a new `Behavior` without wrapping the body in a function ourselves:

```
(def time-behavior (behavior (System/nanoTime)))

@time-behavior
;; 201003153977194

@time-behavior
;; 201005133457949
```

In the preceding example, we defined `time-behavior` that always contains the current system time. We can then turn this behavior into a stream of discrete events by using the `sample` function:

```
(def time-stream (sample time-behavior 1500))
(def token        (subscribe time-stream #(prn "Time is " %)))
;; "Time is " 201668521217402
;; "Time is " 201670030219351
;; ...

(dispose token)
```

> Always remember to keep a reference to the subscription token when dealing with infinite streams such as the ones created by `sample` and `from-interval`, or else you might incur undesired memory leaks.

Congratulations! We have a working, minimal CES framework using `core.async`!

We didn't prove it works with ClojureScript, however, which was one of the main requirements early on. That's okay. We will be tackling that soon by developing a simple ClojureScript application, which makes use of our new framework.

In order to do this, we need to deploy the framework to our local Maven repository. From the project root, type the following `lein` command:

```
$ lein install
Rewriting src/cljx to target/classes (clj) with features #{clj} and 0
transformations.
Rewriting src/cljx to target/classes (cljs) with features #{cljs} and 1
transformations.
Created respondent/target/respondent-0.1.0-SNAPSHOT.jar
Wrote respondent/pom.xml
```

Exercises

The following sections have a few exercises for you.

Exercise 5.1

Extend our current `EventStream` implementation to include a function called `take`. It works much like Clojure's core `take` function for sequences: it will take n items from the underlying event stream after which it will stop emitting items.

A sample interaction, which takes the first five items emitted from the original event stream, is shown here:

```
(def es1 (from-interval 500))
(def take-es (take es1 5))

(subscribe take-es #(prn "Take values: " %))

;; "Take values: " 0
;; "Take values: " 1
;; "Take values: " 2
;; "Take values: " 3
;; "Take values: " 4
```

Keeping some state might be useful here. Atoms can help. Additionally, try to think of a way to dispose of any unwanted subscriptions required by the solution.

Exercise 5.2

In this exercise, we will add a function called `zip` that zips together items emitted from two different event streams into a vector.

A sample interaction with the `zip` function is as follows:

```
(def es1 (from-interval 500))
(def es2 (map (from-interval 500) #(* % 2)))
(def zipped (zip es1 es2))

(def token (subscribe zipped #(prn "Zipped values: " %)))

;; "Zipped values: " [0 0]
;; "Zipped values: " [1 2]
;; "Zipped values: " [2 4]
;; "Zipped values: " [3 6]
;; "Zipped values: " [4 8]

(dispose token)
```

For this exercise, we need a way to know when we have enough items to emit from both event streams. Managing this internal state can be tricky at first. Clojure's `ref` types and, in particular, `dosync`, can be of use.

A respondent application

This chapter would not be complete if we didn't go through the whole development life cycle of deploying and using the new framework in a new application. This is the purpose of this section.

The application we will build is extremely simple. All it does is track the position of the mouse using the reactive primitives we built into respondent.

To that end, we will be using the excellent lein template `cljs-start` (see `https://github.com/magomimmo/cljs-start`), created by Mimmo Cosenza to help developers get started with ClojureScript.

Let's get started:

```
lein new cljs-start respondent-app
```

Next, let's modify the project file to include the following dependencies:

```
[clojure-reactive-programming/respondent "0.1.0-SNAPSHOT"]
[prismatic/dommy "0.1.2"]
```

The first dependency is self-explanatory. It's simply our own framework. `dommy` is a DOM manipulation library for ClojureScript. We'll briefly use it when building our web page.

Next, edit the `dev-resources/public/index.html` file to match the following:

```
<!doctype html>
<html lang="en">
<head>
    <meta charset="utf-8">

    <title>Example: tracking mouse position</title>
    <!--[if lt IE 9]>
    <script src="http://html5shiv.googlecode.com/svn/trunk/html5.
js"></script>
    <![endif]-->
</head>

<body>
    <div id="test">
        <h1>Mouse (x,y) coordinates:</h1>
    </div>
    <div id="mouse-xy">
      (0,0)
```

```
    </div>
    <script src="js/respondent_app.js"></script>
  </body>
</html>
```

In the preceding snippet, we created a new `div` element, which will contain the mouse position. It defaults to `(0,0)`.

The last piece of the puzzle is modifying `src/cljs/respondent_app/core.cljs` to match the following:

```
(ns respondent-app.core
  (:require [respondent.core :as r]
            [dommy.core :as dommy])
  (:use-macros
   [dommy.macros :only [sel1]]))


(def mouse-pos-stream (r/event-stream))
(set! (.-onmousemove js/document)
      (fn [e]
        (r/deliver mouse-pos-stream [(.-pageX e) (.-pageY e)])))

(r/subscribe mouse-pos-stream
             (fn [[x y]]
               (dommy/set-text! (sel1 :#mouse-xy)
                                (str "(" x "," y ")"))))
```

This is our main application logic. It creates an event stream to which we deliver the current mouse position from the `onmousemove` event of the browser window.

Later, we simply subscribe to it and use `dommy` to select and set the text of the `div` element we added previously.

We are now ready to use the app! Let's start by compiling ClojureScript:

$ lein compile

This should take a few seconds. If all is well, the next thing to do is to start a REPL session and start up the server:

$ lein repl
user=> (run)

Now, point your browser to `http://localhost:3000/` and drag the mouse around to see its current position.

Congratulations on successfully developing, deploying, and using your own CES framework!

CES versus core.async

At this stage, you might be wondering when you should choose one approach over the other. After all, as demonstrated at the beginning of this chapter, we could use core.async to do everything we have done using respondent.

It all comes down to using the right level of abstraction for the task at hand.

core.async gives us many low level primitives that are extremely useful when working with processes, which need to talk to each other. The core.async channels work as concurrent blocking queues and are an excellent synchronization mechanism in these scenarios.

However, it makes other solutions harder to implement: for instance, channels are single-take by default, so if we have multiple consumers interested in the values put inside a channel, we have to implement the distribution ourselves using tools such as mult and tap.

CES frameworks, on the other hand, operate at a higher level of abstraction and work with multiple subscribers by default.

Additionally, core.async relies on side effects, as can be seen by the use of functions such as >! inside go blocks. Frameworks such as RxClojure promote stream transformations by the use of pure functions.

This is not to say there aren't side effects in CES frameworks. There most definitely are. However, as a consumer of the library, this is mostly hidden from our eyes, allowing us to think of most of our code as simple sequence transformations.

In conclusion, different application domains will benefit more or less from either approach—sometimes they can benefit from both. We should think hard about our application domain and analyze the types of solutions and idioms developers are most likely to design. This will point us in the direction of better abstraction for whatever application we are developing at a given time.

Summary

In this chapter, we developed our very own CES framework. By developing our own framework, we have solidified our understanding of both CES and how to effectively use `core.async`.

The idea that `core.async` could be used as the foundation of a CES framework isn't mine, however. James Reeves (see `https://github.com/weavejester`)—creator of the routing library **Compojure** (see `https://github.com/weavejester/compojure`) and many other useful Clojure libraries—also saw the same potential and set off to write **Reagi** (see `https://github.com/weavejester/reagi`), a CES library built on top of `core.async`, similar in spirit to the one we developed in this chapter.

He has put a lot more effort into it, making it a more robust option for a pure Clojure framework. We'll be looking at it in the next chapter.

6
Building a Simple ClojureScript Game with Reagi

In the previous chapter, we learned how a framework for **Compositional Event Systems** (CES) works by building our own framework, which we called *respondent*. It gave us a great insight into the main abstractions involved in such a piece of software as well as a good overview of core.async, Clojure's library for asynchronous programming and the foundation of our framework.

Respondent is but a toy framework, however. We paid little attention to cross-cutting concerns such as memory efficiency and exception handling. That is okay as we used it as a vehicle for learning more about handling and composing event systems with core.async. Additionally, its design is intentionally similar to Reagi's design.

In this chapter, we will:

- Learn about Reagi, a CES framework built on top of core.async
- Use Reagi to build the rudiments of a ClojureScript game that will teach us how to handle user input in a clean and maintainable way
- Briefly compare Reagi to other CES frameworks and get a feel for when to use each one

Setting up the project

Have you ever played Asteroids? If you haven't, Asteroids is an arcade space shooter first released by Atari in 1979. In Asteroids, you are the pilot of a ship flying through space. As you do so, you get surrounded by asteroids and flying saucers you have to shoot and destroy.

Developing the whole game in one chapter is too ambitious and would distract us from the subject of this book. We will limit ourselves to making sure we have a ship on the screen we can fly around as well as shoot space bullets into the void. By the end of this chapter, we will have something that looks like what is shown in the following screenshot:

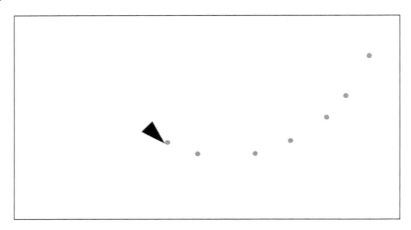

To get started, we will create a newClojureScript project using the same leiningen template we used in the previous chapter, cljs-start (see https://github.com/magomimmo/cljs-start):

lein new cljs-start reagi-game

Next, add the following dependencies to your project file:

```
[org.clojure/clojurescript "0.0-2138"]
[reagi "0.10.0"]
[rm-hull/monet "0.1.12"]
```

The last dependency, monet (see https://github.com/rm-hull/monet), is a ClojureScript library you can use to work with HTML 5 Canvas. It is a high-level wrapper on top of the Canvas API and makes interacting with it a lot simpler.

Before we continue, it's probably a good idea to make sure our setup is working properly. Change into the project directory, start a Clojure REPL, and then start the embedded web server:

```
cd reagi-game/
lein repl
Compiling ClojureScript.
Compiling "dev-resources/public/js/reagi_game.js" from ("src/cljs" "test/
cljs" "dev-resources/tools/repl")...
user=> (run)
2014-06-14 19:21:40.381:INFO:oejs.Server:jetty-7.6.8.v20121106
2014-06-14 19:21:40.403:INFO:oejs.AbstractConnector:Started
SelectChannelConnector@0.0.0.0:3000
#<Server org.eclipse.jetty.server.Server@51f6292b>
```

This will compile the ClojureScript source files to JavaScript and start the sample web server. In your browser, navigate to `http://localhost:3000/`. If you see something like the following, we are good to go:

ClojureScript

Welcome to ClojureScript!

As we will be working with HTML 5 Canvas, we need an actual canvas to render to. Let's update our HTML document to include that. It's located under `dev-resources/public/index.html`:

```
<!doctype html>
<html lang="en">
  <head>
    <meta charset="utf-8">
    <title>bREPL Connection</title>
    <!--[if lt IE 9]>
        <script src="http://html5shiv.googlecode.com/svn/trunk/html5.
js"></script>
        <![endif]-->
  </head>

  <body>
    <canvas id="canvas" width="800" height="600"></canvas>
    <script src="js/reagi_game.js"></script>
```

```
    </body>
</html>
```

We have added a `canvas` DOM element to our document. All rendering will happen in this context.

Game entities

Our game will have only two entities: one representing the spaceship and the other representing bullets. To better organize the code, we will put all entity-related code in its own file, `src/cljs/reagi_game/entities.cljs`. This file will also contain some of the rendering logic, so we'll need to require `monet`:

```
(ns reagi-game.entities
  (:require [monet.canvas :as canvas]
            [monet.geometry :as geom]))
```

Next, we'll add a few helper functions to avoid repeating ourselves too much:

```
(defn shape-x [shape]
  (-> shape :pos deref :x))

(defn shape-y [shape]
  (-> shape :pos deref :y))

(defn shape-angle [shape]
  @(:angle shape))


(defn shape-data [x y angle]
  {:pos   (atom {:x x :y y})
   :angle (atom angle)})
```

The first three functions are simply a shorter way of getting data out of our shape data structure. The `shape-data` function creates a structure. Note that we are using `atom`s, one of Clojure's reference types, to represent a shape's position and angle.

This way, we can safely pass our shape data into monet's rendering functions and still be able to update it in a consistent way.

Next up is our ship constructor function. This is where the bulk of the interaction with monet happens:

```
(defn ship-entity [ship]
  (canvas/entity {:x (shape-x ship)
```

```
          :y (shape-y ship)
          :angle (shape-angle ship)}
         (fn [value]
           (-> value
               (assoc :x      (shape-x ship))
               (assoc :y      (shape-y ship))
               (assoc :angle (shape-angle ship))))
         (fn [ctx val]
           (-> ctx
               canvas/save
               (canvas/translate (:x val) (:y val))
               (canvas/rotate (:angle val))
               (canvas/begin-path)
               (canvas/move-to 50 0)
               (canvas/line-to 0 -15)
               (canvas/line-to 0 15)
               (canvas/fill)
               canvas/restore))))
```

There is quite a bit going on, so let's break it down.

canvas/entity is a monet constructor and expects you to provide three arguments
that describe our ship: its initial x, y coordinates and angle, an update function that
gets called in the draw loop, and a draw function that is responsible for actually
drawing the shape onto the screen after each update.

The update function is fairly straightforward:

```
(fn [value]
  (-> value
      (assoc :x      (shape-x ship))
      (assoc :y      (shape-y ship))
      (assoc :angle (shape-angle ship))))
```

We simply update its attributes to the current values from the ship's atoms.

The next function, responsible for drawing, interacts with monet's API more heavily:

```
(fn [ctx val]
  (-> ctx
      canvas/save
      (canvas/translate (:x val) (:y val))
      (canvas/rotate (:angle val))
      (canvas/begin-path)
      (canvas/move-to 50 0)
```

```
(canvas/line-to 0 -15)
(canvas/line-to 0 15)
(canvas/fill)
canvas/restore))
```

We start by saving the current context so that we can restore things such as drawing style and canvas positioning later. Next, we translate the canvas to the ship's x,y coordinates and rotate it according to its angle. We then start drawing our shape, a triangle, and finish by restoring our saved context.

The next function also creates an entity, our bullet:

```
(declare move-forward!)

(defn make-bullet-entity [monet-canvas key shape]
  (canvas/entity {:x (shape-x shape)
                  :y (shape-y shape)
                  :angle (shape-angle shape)}
                 (fn [value]
                   (when (not
                           (geom/contained?
                             {:x 0 :y 0
                              :w (.-width (:canvas monet-canvas))
                              :h (.-height (:canvas monet-canvas))}
                             {:x (shape-x shape)
                              :y (shape-y shape)
                              :r 5}))
                     (canvas/remove-entity monet-canvas key))
                   (move-forward! shape)
                   (-> value
                       (assoc :x     (shape-x shape))
                       (assoc :y     (shape-y shape))
                       (assoc :angle (shape-angle shape))))
                 (fn [ctx val]
                   (-> ctx
                       canvas/save
                       (canvas/translate (:x val) (:y val))
                       (canvas/rotate (:angle val))
                       (canvas/fill-style "red")
                       (canvas/circle {:x 10 :y 0 :r 5})
                       canvas/restore))))
```

As before, let's inspect the update and drawing functions. We'll start with update:

```
(fn [value]
  (when (not
          (geom/contained?
           {:x 0 :y 0
            :w (.-width (:canvas monet-canvas))
            :h (.-height (:canvas monet-canvas))}
           {:x (shape-x shape)
            :y (shape-y shape)
            :r 5}))
    (canvas/remove-entity monet-canvas key))
  (move-forward! shape)
  (-> value
      (assoc :x     (shape-x shape))
      (assoc :y     (shape-y shape))
      (assoc :angle (shape-angle shape)))))
```

Bullets have a little more logic in their update function. As you fire them from the ship, we might create hundreds of these entities, so it's a good practice to get rid of them as soon as they go off the visible canvas area. That's the first thing the function does: it uses geom/contained? to check whether the entity is within the dimensions of the canvas, removing it when it isn't.

Different from the ship, however, bullets don't need user input in order to move. Once fired, they move on their own. That's why the next thing we do is call move-forward! We haven't implemented this function yet, so we had to declare it beforehand. We'll get to it.

Once the bullet's coordinates and angle have been updated, we simply return the new entity.

The draw function is a bit simpler than the ship's version mostly due to its shape being simpler; it's just a red circle:

```
(fn [ctx val]
                    (-> ctx
                        canvas/save
                        (canvas/translate (:x val) (:y val))
                        (canvas/rotate (:angle val))
                        (canvas/fill-style "red")
                        (canvas/circle {:x 10 :y 0 :r 5})
                        canvas/restore))
```

Now, we'll move on to the functions responsible for updating our shape's coordinates and angle, starting with move!:

```
(def speed 200)

(defn calculate-x [angle]
  (* speed (/ (* (Math/cos angle)
                 Math/PI)
              180)))

(defn calculate-y [angle]
  (* speed (/ (* (Math/sin angle)
                 Math/PI)
              180)))

(defn move! [shape f]
  (let [pos (:pos shape)]
    (swap! pos (fn [xy]
                 (-> xy
                     (update-in [:x]
                                #(f % (calculate-x
                                        (shape-angle shape)))))
                     (update-in [:y]
                                #(f % (calculate-y
                                        (shape-angle shape)))))))))
```

To keep things simple, both the ship and bullets use the same speed value to calculate their positioning, here defined as 200.

move! takes two arguments: the shape map and a function f. This function will either be the + (plus) or the - (minus) function, depending on whether we're moving forward or backward, respectively. Next, it updates the shape's x,y coordinates using some basic trigonometry.

If you're wondering why we are passing the plus and minus functions as arguments, it's all about not repeating ourselves, as the next two functions show:

```
(defn move-forward! [shape]
  (move! shape +))

(defn move-backward! [shape]
  (move! shape -))
```

With movement taken care of, the next step is to write the rotation functions:

```
(defn rotate! [shape f]
  (swap! (:angle shape) #(f % (/ (/ Math/PI 3) 20)))))

(defn rotate-right! [shape]
  (rotate! shape +))

(defn rotate-left! [shape]
  (rotate! shape -))
```

So far, we've got ship movement covered! But what good is our ship if we can't fire bullets? Let's make sure we have that covered as well:

```
(defn fire! [monet-canvas ship]
  (let [entity-key (keyword (gensym "bullet"))
        data (shape-data (shape-x ship)
                         (shape-y ship)
                         (shape-angle ship))
        bullet (make-bullet-entity monet-canvas
                                   entity-key
                                   data)]
    (canvas/add-entity monet-canvas entity-key bullet)))
```

The `fire!` function takes two arguments: a reference to the game canvas and the ship. It then creates a new bullet by calling `make-bullet-entity` and adds it to the canvas.

Note how we use Clojure's `gensym` function to create a unique key for the new entity. We use this key to remove an entity from the game.

This concludes the code for the `entities` namespace.

 gensym is quite heavily used in writing hygienic macros as you can be sure that the generated symbols will not clash with any local bindings belonging to the code using the macro. Macros are beyond the scope of this book, but you might find this series of macro exercises useful in the learning process, at https://github.com/leonardoborges/clojure-macros-workshop.

Putting it all together

We're now ready to assemble our game. Go ahead and open the core namespace file, `src/cljs/reagi_game/core.cljs`, and add the following:

```
(ns reagi-game.core
  (:require [monet.canvas :as canvas]
            [reagi.core :as r]
            [clojure.set :as set]
            [reagi-game.entities :as entities
             :refer [move-forward! move-backward! rotate-left! rotate-
right! fire!]]]))
```

The following snippet sets up various data structures and references we'll need in order to develop the game:

```
(def canvas-dom (.getElementById js/document "canvas"))

(def monet-canvas (canvas/init canvas-dom "2d"))

(def ship
      (entities/shape-data (/ (.-width (:canvas monet-canvas)) 2)
                           (/ (.-height (:canvas monet-canvas)) 2)
                           0))

(def ship-entity (entities/ship-entity ship))

(canvas/add-entity monet-canvas :ship-entity ship-entity)
(canvas/draw-loop monet-canvas)
```

We start by creating `monet-canvas` from a reference to our `canvas` DOM element. We then create our ship data, placing it at the center of the canvas, and add the entity to `monet-canvas`. Finally, we start a draw-loop, which will handle our animations using the browser's native capabilities—internally it calls `window.requestAnimationFrame()`, if available, but it falls back to `window.setTimemout()` otherwise.

If you were to try the application now, this would be enough to draw the ship on the middle of the screen, but nothing else would happen as we haven't started handling user input yet.

As far as user input goes, we're concerned with a few actions:

- Ship movement: rotation, forward, and backward
- Firing the ship's gun
- Pausing the game

To account for these actions, we'll define some constants that represent the ASCII codes of the keys involved:

```
(def UP    38)
(def RIGHT 39)
(def DOWN  40)
(def LEFT  37)
(def FIRE  32) ;; space
(def PAUSE 80) ;; lower-case P
```

This should look sensible as we are using the keys traditionally used for these types of actions.

Modeling user input as event streams

One of the things discussed in the earlier chapters is that if you can think of events as a list of things that haven't happened yet; you can probably model it as an event stream. In our case, this list is composed by the keys the player presses during the game and can be visualized like so:

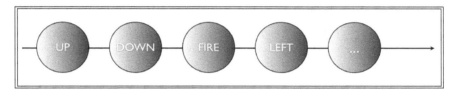

There is a catch though. Most games need to handle simultaneously pressed keys.

Say you're flying the spaceship forwards. You don't want to have to stop it in order to rotate it to the left and then continue moving forwards. What you want is to press left at the same time you're pressing up and have the ship respond accordingly.

This hints at the fact that we need to be able to tell whether the player is currently pressing multiple keys. Traditionally this is done in JavaScript by keeping track of which keys are being held down in a map-like object, using flags. Something similar to the following snippet:

```
var keysPressed = {};

document.addEventListener('keydown', function(e) {
    keysPressed[e.keyCode] = true;
}, false);
document.addEventListener('keyup', function(e) {
    keysPressed[e.keyCode] = false;
}, false);
```

Then, later in the game loop, you would check whether there are multiple keys being pressed:

```
function gameLoop() {
    if (keyPressed[UP] && keyPressed[LEFT]) {
        // update ship position
    }
    // ...
}
```

While this code works, it relies on mutating the `keysPressed` object which isn't ideal.

Additionally, with a setup similar to the preceding one, the `keysPressed` object is global to the application as it is needed both in the `keyup`/`keydown` event handlers as well as in the game loop itself.

In functional programming, we strive to eliminate or reduce the amount of global mutable state in order to write readable, maintainable code that is less error-prone. We will apply these principles here.

As seen in the preceding JavaScript example, we can register callbacks to be notified whenever a `keyup` or `keydown` event happens. This is useful as we can easily turn them into event streams:

```
(defn keydown-stream []
  (let [out (r/events)]
    (set! (.-onkeydown js/document)
          #(r/deliver out [::down (.-keyCode %)])))
    out))

(defn keyup-stream []
  (let [out (r/events)]
    (set! (.-onkeyup   js/document)
          #(r/deliver out [::up (.-keyCode %)])))
    out))
```

Both `keydown-stream` and `keyup-stream` return a new stream to which they deliver events whenever they happen. Each event is tagged with a keyword, so we can easily identify its type.

We would like to handle both types of events simultaneously and as such we need a way to combine these two streams into a single one.

There are many ways in which we can combine streams, for example, using operators such as `zip` and `flatmap`. For this instance, however, we are interested in the `merge` operator. `merge` creates a new stream that emits values from both streams as they arrive:

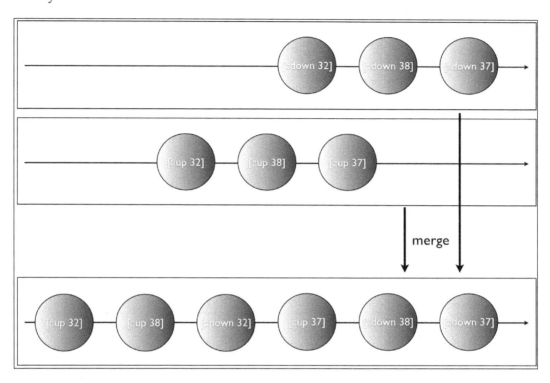

This gives us enough to start creating our stream of active keys. Based on what we have discussed so far, our stream looks something like the following at the moment:

```
(def active-keys-stream
  (->> (r/merge (keydown-stream) (keyup-stream))
    ...
    ))
```

To keep track of which keys are currently pressed, we will use a ClojureScript set. This way we don't have to worry about setting flags to true or false—we can simply perform standard set operations and add/remove keys from the data structure.

The next thing we need is a way to accumulate the pressed keys into this set as new events are emitted from the merged stream.

In functional programming, whenever we wish to accumulate or aggregate some type of data over a sequence of values, we use `reduce`.

Most — if not all — CES frameworks have this function built-in. RxJava calls it `scan`. Reagi, on the other hand, calls it `reduce`, making it intuitive to functional programmers in general.

That is the function we will use to finish the implementation of `active-keys-stream`:

```
(def active-keys-stream
  (->> (r/merge (keydown-stream) (keyup-stream))
       (r/reduce (fn [acc [event-type key-code]]
           (condp = event-type
               ::down (conj acc key-code)
               ::up (disj acc key-code)
               acc))
         #{})
       (r/sample 25)))
```

`r/reduce` takes three arguments: a reducing function, an optional initial/seed value, and the stream to reduce over.

Our seed value is an empty set as initially the user hasn't yet pressed any keys. Then, our reducing function checks the event type, removing or adding the key from/to the set as appropriate.

As a result, what we have is a stream like the one represented as follows:

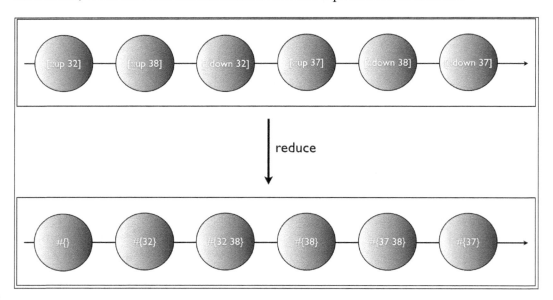

Working with the active keys stream

The ground work we've done so far will make sure we can easily handle game events in a clean and maintainable way. The main idea behind having a stream representing the game keys is that now we can partition it much like we would a normal list.

For instance, if we're interested in all events where the key pressed is UP, we would run the following code:

```
(->> active-keys-stream
     (r/filter (partial some #{UP}))
     (r/map (fn [_] (.log js/console "Pressed up..."))))
```

Similarly, for events involving the FIRE key, we could do the following:

```
(->> active-keys-stream

     (r/filter (partial some #{FIRE}))
     (r/map (fn [_] (.log js/console "Pressed fire..."))))
```

This works because in Clojure, sets can be used as predicates. We can quickly verify this at the REPL:

```
user> (def numbers #{12 13 14})
#'user/numbers
user> (some #{12} numbers)
12
user> (some #{15} numbers)
nil
```

By representing the events as a stream, we can easily operate on them using familiar sequence functions such as map and filter.

Writing code like this, however, is a little repetitive. The two previous examples are pretty much saying something along these lines: filter all events matching a given predicate pred and then map the f function over them. We can abstract this pattern in a function we'll call filter-map:

```
(defn filter-map [pred f & args]
  (->> active-keys-stream
       (r/filter (partial some pred))
       (r/map (fn [_] (apply f args)))))
```

With this helper function in place, it becomes easy to handle our game actions:

```
(filter-map #{FIRE}  fire! monet-canvas ship)
(filter-map #{UP}    move-forward!  ship)
(filter-map #{DOWN}  move-backward! ship)
(filter-map #{RIGHT} rotate-right!  ship)
(filter-map #{LEFT}  rotate-left!   ship)
```

The only thing missing now is taking care of pausing the animations when the player presses the PAUSE key. We follow the same logic as above, but with a slight change:

```
(defn pause! [_]
  (if @(:updating? monet-canvas)
    (canvas/stop-updating monet-canvas)
    (canvas/start-updating monet-canvas)))

(->> active-keys-stream
     (r/filter (partial some #{PAUSE}))
     (r/throttle 100)
     (r/map pause!))
```

Monet makes a flag available that tells us whether it is currently updating the animation state. We use that as a cheap mechanism to "pause" the game.

Note that active-keys-stream pushes events as they happen so, if a user is holding a button down for any amount of time, we will get multiple events for that key. As such, we would probably get multiple occurrences of the PAUSE key in a very short amount of time. This would cause the game to frantically stop/start. In order to prevent this from happening, we throttle the filtered stream and ignore all PAUSE events that happen in a window shorter than 100 milliseconds.

To make sure we didn't miss anything, this is what our src/cljs/reagi_game/ core.cljs file should look like, in full:

```
(ns reagi-game.core
  (:require [monet.canvas :as canvas]
            [reagi.core :as r]
            [clojure.set :as set]
            [reagi-game.entities :as entities
             :refer [move-forward! move-backward! rotate-left! rotate-
right! fire!]]))

(def canvas-dom (.getElementById js/document "canvas"))

(def monet-canvas (canvas/init canvas-dom "2d"))
```

```
(def ship (entities/shape-data (/ (.-width (:canvas monet-canvas)) 2)
                               (/ (.-height (:canvas monet-canvas)) 2)
                               0))

(def ship-entity (entities/ship-entity ship))

(canvas/add-entity monet-canvas :ship-entity ship-entity)
(canvas/draw-loop monet-canvas)

(def UP    38)
(def RIGHT 39)
(def DOWN  40)
(def LEFT  37)
(def FIRE  32) ;; space
(def PAUSE 80) ;; lower-case P

(defn keydown-stream []
  (let [out (r/events)]
    (set! (.-onkeydown js/document) #(r/deliver out [::down (.-keyCode
%)]))
    out))

(defn keyup-stream []
  (let [out (r/events)]
    (set! (.-onkeyup  js/document) #(r/deliver out [::up (.-keyCode
%)]))
    out))

(def active-keys-stream
  (->> (r/merge (keydown-stream) (keyup-stream))
       (r/reduce (fn [acc [event-type key-code]]
           (condp = event-type
               ::down (conj acc key-code)
               ::up (disj acc key-code)
               acc))
           #{})
       (r/sample 25)))

(defn filter-map [pred f & args]
  (->> active-keys-stream
       (r/filter (partial some pred))
       (r/map (fn [_] (apply f args)))))

(filter-map #{FIRE}  fire! monet-canvas ship)
(filter-map #{UP}    move-forward!  ship)
```

```
(filter-map #{DOWN}  move-backward! ship)
(filter-map #{RIGHT} rotate-right!  ship)
(filter-map #{LEFT}  rotate-left!   ship)

(defn pause! [_]
  (if @(:updating? monet-canvas)
    (canvas/stop-updating monet-canvas)
    (canvas/start-updating monet-canvas)))

(->> active-keys-stream
     (r/filter (partial some #{PAUSE}))
     (r/throttle 100)
     (r/map pause!))
```

This completes the code and we're now ready to have a look at the results.

If you still have the server running from earlier in this chapter, simply exit the REPL, start it again, and start the embedded web server:

```
lein repl
Compiling ClojureScript.
Compiling "dev-resources/public/js/reagi_game.js" from ("src/cljs" "test/
cljs" "dev-resources/tools/repl")...
user=> (run)
2014-06-14 19:21:40.381:INFO:oejs.Server:jetty-7.6.8.v20121106
2014-06-14 19:21:40.403:INFO:oejs.AbstractConnector:Started
SelectChannelConnector@0.0.0.0:3000
#<Server org.eclipse.jetty.server.Server@51f6292b>
```

This will compile the latest version of our ClojureScript source to JavaScript.

Alternatively, you can leave the REPL running and simply ask `cljsbuild` to auto-compile the source code from another terminal window:

```
lein cljsbuild auto
Compiling "dev-resources/public/js/reagi_game.js" from ("src/cljs" "test/
cljs" "dev-resources/tools/repl")...
Successfully compiled "dev-resources/public/js/reagi_game.js" in 13.23869
seconds.
```

Now you can point your browser to `http://localhost:3000/` and fly around your spaceship! Don't forget to shoot some bullets as well!

Reagi and other CES frameworks

Back in *Chapter 4*, *Introduction to core.async*, we had an overview of the main differences between `core.async` and CES. Another question that might have arisen in this chapter is this: how do we decide which CES framework to use?

The answer is less clear than before and often depends on the specifics of the tool being looked at. We have learned about two such tools so far: Reactive Extensions (encompassing RxJS, RxJava, and RxClojure) and Reagi.

Reactive Extensions (Rx) is a much more mature framework. Its first version for the .NET platform was released in 2011 and the ideas in it have since evolved substantially.

Additionally, ports for other platforms such as RxJava are being heavily used in production by big names such as Netflix.

A drawback of Rx is that if you would like to use it both in the browser and on the server, you have to use two separate frameworks, RxJS and RxJava, respectively. While they do share the same API, they are different codebases, which can incur bugs that might have been solved in one port but not yet in another.

For Clojure developers, it also means relying more on interoperability to interact with the full API of Rx.

Reagi, on the other hand, is a new player in this space but builds on the solid foundation laid out by `core.async`. It is fully developed in Clojure and solves the in-browser/on-server issue by compiling to both Clojure and ClojureScript.

Reagi also allows seamless integration with `core.async` via functions such as `port` and `subscribe`, which allow channels to be created from event streams.

Moreover, the use of `core.async` in ClojureScript applications is becoming ubiquitous, so chances are you already have it as a dependency. This makes Reagi an attractive option for the times when we need a higher level of abstraction than the one provided by `core.async`.

Summary

In this chapter, we learned how we can use the techniques from reactive programming we have learned so far in order to write code that is cleaner and easier to maintain. To do so, we insisted on thinking about asynchronous events simply as lists and saw how that way of thinking lends itself quite easily to being modeled as an event stream. All our game has to do, then, is operate on these streams using familiar sequence processing functions.

We also learned the basics of Reagi, a framework for CES similar to the one we created in *Chapter 4, Introduction to core.async*, but that is more feature rich and robust.

In the next chapter, we will take a break from CES and see how a more traditional reactive approach based on data flows can be useful.

7
The UI as a Function

So far we have taken a journey through managing complexity by efficiently handling and modeling asynchronous workflows in terms of streams of data. In particular, *Chapter 4*, *Introduction to core.async* and *Chapter 5*, *Creating Your Own CES Framework with core.async* explored what's involved in libraries that provide primitives and combinators for **Compositional Event Systems**. We also built a simple ClojureScript application that made use of our framework.

One thing you might have noticed is that none of the examples so far have dealt with what happens to the data once we are ready to present it to our users. It's still an open question that we, as application developers, need to answer.

In this chapter, we will look at one way to handle Reactive User Interfaces in web applications using React (see `http://facebook.github.io/react/`), a modern JavaScript framework developed by Facebook, as well as:

- Learn how React renders user interfaces efficiently
- Be introduced to Om, a ClojureScript interface to React
- Learn how Om leverages persistent data structures for performance
- Develop two fully working ClojureScript applications with Om, including the use of `core.async` for intercomponent communication

The problem with complex web UIs

With the rise of single-page web applications, it became a must to be able to manage the growth and complexity of a JavaScript codebase. The same applies to ClojureScript.

In an effort to manage this complexity, a plethora of JavaScript MVC frameworks have emerged such as AngularJS, Backbone.js, Ember.js, and KnockoutJS to name a few.

They are very different, but share a few common features:

- Give single-page applications more structure by providing models, views, controllers, templates, and so on
- Provide client-side routing
- Two-way data binding

In this chapter, we'll be focusing on the last goal.

Two-way data binding is absolutely crucial if we are to develop even a moderately complex single-page web application. Here's how it works.

Suppose we're developing a phone book application. More than likely, we will have a model — or entity, map, what have you — that represents a contact. The contact model might have attributes such as name, phone number, and e-mail address.

Of course, this application would not be all that useful if users couldn't update contact information, so we will need a form which displays the current details for a contact and lets you update the contact's information.

The contact model might have been loaded via an AJAX request and then might have used explicit DOM manipulation code to display the form. This would look something like the following pseudo-code:

```
function editContact(contactId) {
  contactService.get(contactId, function(data) {
    contactForm.setName(data.name);
    contactForm.setPhone(data.phone);
    contactForm.setEmail(data.email);
  })
}
```

But what happens when the user updates someone's information? We need to store it somehow. On clicking on save, a function such as the following would do the trick, assuming you're using jQuery:

```
$("save-button").click(function(){
  contactService.update(contactForm.serialize(), function(){
    flashMessage.set("Contact Updated.")
  })
```

This seemingly harmless code poses a big problem. The contact model for this particular person is now out of date. If we were still developing web applications the old way, where we reload the page at every update, this wouldn't be a problem. However, the whole point of single-page web applications is to be responsive, so it keeps a lot of state on the client, and it is important to keep our models synced with our views.

This is where two-way data binding comes in. An example from AngularJS would look like the following:

```
// JS
// in the Controller
$scope.contact = {
  name: 'Leonardo Borges',
  phone '+61 xxx xxx xxx',
  email: 'leonardoborges.rj@gmail.com'
}


<!-- HTML -->
<!-- in the View -->
<form>
  <input type="text" name="contactName"  ng-model="contact.name"/>
  <input type="text" name="contactPhone" ng-model="contact.phone"/>
  <input type="text" name="contactEmail" ng-model="contact.email"/>
</form>
```

Angular isn't the target of this chapter, so I won't dig into the details. All we need to know from this example is that `$scope` is how we tell Angular to make our contact model available to our views. In the view, the custom attribute `ng-model` tells Angular to look up that property in the scope. This establishes a two-way relationship in such a way that when your model data changes in the scope, Angular refreshes the UI. Similarly, if the user edits the form, Angular updates the model, keeping everything in sync.

There are, however, two main problems with this approach:

- It can be slow. The way Angular and friends implement two-way data binding is, roughly speaking, by attaching event handlers and watchers to view both custom- attributes and model attributes. For complex enough user interfaces, you will start noticing that the UI becomes slower to render, diminishing the user experience.

- It relies heavily on mutation. As functional programmers, we strive to limit side effects to a minimum.

The slowness that comes with this and similar approaches is two-fold: firstly, AngularJS and friends have to "watch" all properties of every model in the scope in order to track updates. Once the framework determines that data has changed in the model, it then looks up parts of the UI, which depend on that information — such as the fragments using `ng-model` above — and then it re-renders them.

Secondly, the DOM is the slowest part of most single-page web applications. If we think about it for a moment, these frameworks are triggering dozens or perhaps hundreds of DOM event handlers in order to keep the data in sync, each of which ends up updating a node — or several — in the DOM.

Don't take my word for it though. I ran a simple benchmark to compare a pure calculation versus locating a DOM element and updating its value to the result of the said calculation. Here are the results — I've used JSPerf to run the benchmark, and these results are for Chrome 37.0.2062.94 on Mac OS X Mavericks (see `http://jsperf.com/purefunctions-vs-dom`):

```
document.getElementsByName("sum")[0].value = 1 + 2
// Operations per second: 2,090,202

1 + 2
// Operations per second: 780,538,120
```

Updating the DOM is orders of magnitude slower than performing a simple calculation. It seems logical that we would want to do this in the most efficient manner possible.

However, if we don't keep our data in sync, we're back at square one. There should be a way by which we can drastically reduce the amount of rendering being done, while retaining the convenience of two-way data binding. Can we have our cake and eat it too?

Enter React.js

As we'll see in this chapter, the answer to the question posed in the previous section is a resounding yes and, as you might have guessed, it involves React.js.

But what makes it special?

It's wise to start with what React is not. It is not an MVC framework and as such it is not a replacement for the likes of AngularJS, Backbone.js, and so on. React focuses solely on the V in MVC, and presents a refreshingly different way to think about user interfaces. We must take a slight detour in order to explore how it does that.

Lessons from functional programming

As functional programmers, we don't need to be convinced of the benefits of immutability. We bought into the premise long ago. However, should we not be able to use immutability efficiently, it would not have become commonplace in functional programming languages.

We owe it to the huge amount of research that went into **Purely Functional Data Structures** — first by Okasaki in his book of the same title (see http://www.amazon.com/Purely-Functional-Structures-Chris-Okasaki/dp/0521663504/ref=sr_1_1?ie=UTF8&qid=1409550695&sr=8-1&keywords=purely+functional+data+structures) and then improved by others.

Without it, our programs would be ballooning, both in space and runtime complexity.

The general idea is that given a data structure, the only way to update it is by creating a copy of it with the desired delta applied:

```
(conj [1 2 3] 4)  ;; [1 2 3 4]
```

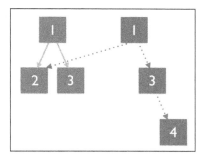

In the preceding image, we have a simplistic view of how `conj` operates. On the left, you have the underlying data structure representing the vector we wish to update. On the right, we have the newly created vector, which, as we can see, shares some structure with the previous vector, as well as containing our new item.

 In reality, the underlying data structure is a tree and the representation was simplified for the purposes of this book. I highly recommend referring to Okasaki's book should the reader want more details on how purely functional data structures work.

Additionally, these functions are considered pure. That is, it relates every input to a single output and does nothing else. This is, in fact, remarkably similar to how React handles user interfaces.

If we think of a UI as a visual representation of a data structure, which reflects the current state of our application, we can, without too much effort, think of UI updates as a simple function whose input is the application state and the output is a DOM representation.

You'll have noticed I didn't say the output is rendering to the DOM — that would make the function impure as rendering is clearly a side effect. It would also make it just as slow as the alternatives.

This DOM representation is essentially a tree of DOM nodes that model how your UI should look, and nothing else.

React calls this representation a **Virtual DOM**, and roughly speaking, instead of watching individual bits and pieces of application state that trigger a DOM re-render upon change, React turns your UI into a function to which you give the whole application state.

When you give this function the new updated state, React renders that state to the Virtual DOM. Remember the Virtual DOM is simply a data structure, so the rendering is extremely fast. Once it's done, React does one of two things:

- It commits the Virtual DOM to the actual DOM if this is the first render.
- Otherwise, it compares the new Virtual DOM with the current Virtual DOM, cached from the previous render of the application. It then uses an efficient diff algorithm to compute the minimum set of changes required to update the real DOM. Finally, it commits this delta to the DOM.

Without digging into the nuts and bolts of React, this is essentially how it is implemented and the reason it is faster than the alternatives. Conceptually, React hits the "refresh" button whenever your application state changes.

Another great benefit is that by thinking of your UI as a function from application state to a Virtual DOM, we recover some of the reasoning we're able to do when working with immutable data structures in functional languages.

In the upcoming sections, we will understand why this is a big win for us Clojure developers.

```
                        :phone "+48 XXX XXX XXX"}}
        :selected-contact-id []
        :editing [false]}))
```

The reason we keep the state in an atom is that Om uses that to re-render the application if we `swap!` or `reset!` it, for instance, if we load some data from the server after the application has been rendered for the first time.

The data in the state itself should be mostly self-explanatory. We have a map containing all contacts, a key representing whether there is currently a contact selected, and a flag that indicates whether we are currently editing the selected contact. What might look odd is that both `:selected-contact-id` and `:editing` keys point to a vector. Just bear with me for a moment; the reason for this will become clear shortly.

Now that we have a draft of our application state, it's time we think about how the state will flow through the different components in our app. A picture is worth a thousand words, so the following diagram shows the high-level architecture through which our data will flow:

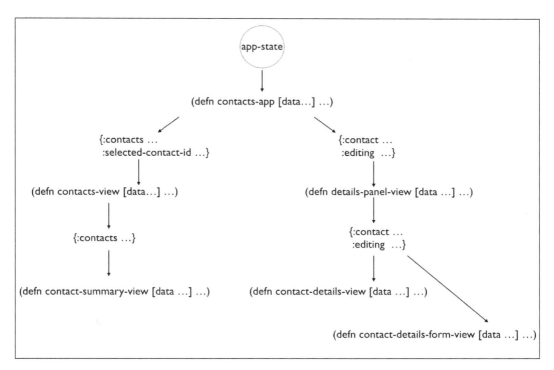

In the preceding image, each function corresponds to an Om component. At the very least, they take some piece of data as their initial state. What is interesting in this image is that as we descend into our more specialized components, they request less state than the main component, `contacts-app`. For instance, the `contacts-view` component needs all contacts as well as the ID of the selected contact. The `details-panel-view` component, on the other hand, only needs the currently selected contact, and whether it's being edited or not. This is a common pattern in Om and we usually want to avoid over-sharing the application state.

With a rough understanding of our high-level architecture, we are ready to start building our Contacts application.

Setting up the Contacts project

Once again, we will use a leiningen template to help us get started. This time we'll be using `om-start` (see `https://github.com/magomimmo/om-start-template`), also by Mimmo Cosenza (see `https://github.com/magomimmo`). Type this in the terminal to create a base project using this template:

```
lein new om-start contacts

cd contacts
```

Next, let's open the `project.clj` file and make sure we have the same versions for the various different dependencies the template pulls in. This is just so that we don't have any surprises with incompatible versions:

```
. . .
  :dependencies [[org.clojure/clojure "1.6.0"]
                 [org.clojure/clojurescript "0.0-2277"]
                 [org.clojure/core.async "0.1.338.0-5c5012-alpha"]
                 [om "0.7.1"]
                 [com.facebook/react "0.11.1"]]
. . .
```

To validate the new project skeleton, still in the terminal, type the following to auto-compile your ClojureScript source files:

```
lein cljsbuild auto
Compiling ClojureScript.
Compiling "dev-resources/public/js/contacts.js" from ("src/cljs" "dev-resources/tools/repl")...
Successfully compiled "dev-resources/public/js/contacts.js" in 9.563 seconds.
```

Now, we should see the template default "Hello World" page if we open the `dev-resources/public/index.html` file in the browser.

Application components

The next thing we'll do is open the `src/cljs/contacts/core.cljs` file, which is where our application code will go, and make sure it looks like the following so that we have a clean slate with the appropriate namespace declaration:

```
(ns contacts.core
  (:require [om.core :as om :include-macros true]
            [om.dom :as dom :include-macros true]))

(enable-console-print!)

(def app-state
  (atom {:contacts {1 {:id    1
                       :name  "James Hetfield"
                       :email "james@metallica.com"
                       :phone "+1 XXX XXX XXX"}
                    2 {:id    2
                       :name  "Adam Darski"
                       :email "the.nergal@behemoth.pl"
                       :phone "+48 XXX XXX XXX"}}
         :selected-contact-id []
         :editing [false]}))

(om/root
  contacts-app
  app-state
  {:target (. js/document (getElementById "app"))})
```

Every Om application starts with a root component created by the `om/root` function. It takes as arguments a function representing a component—`contacts-app`—the initial state of the application—`app-state`—and a map of options of which the only one we care about is `:target`, which tells Om where to mount our root component on the DOM.

In this instance, it will mount on a DOM element whose ID is `app`. This element was given to us by the `om-start` template and is located in the `dev-resources/public/index.html` file.

Of course, this code won't compile yet, as we don't have the `contacts-app` template. Let's solve that and create it above the preceding declaration—we're implementing the components bottom-up:

```
(defn contacts-app [data owner]
  (reify
```

```
  om/IRender
  (render [this]
    (let [[selected-id :as selected-id-cursor]
          (:selected-contact-id data)]
      (dom/div nil
              (om/build contacts-view
                        {:contacts              (:contacts data)
                         :selected-id-cursor selected-id-cursor})
              (om/build details-panel-view
                        {:contact        (get-in data [:contacts
selected-id])
                         :editing-cursor (:editing data)})))))))
```

This snippet introduces a number of new features and terminology, so it deserves a few paragraphs.

When describing om/root, we saw that its first argument must be an Om component. The contact-app function creates one by reifying the om/IRender protocol. This protocol contains a single function — render — which gets called when the application state changes.

Clojure uses reify to implement protocols or Java interfaces on the fly, without the need to create a new type. You can read more about this on the data types page of the Clojure documentation at http://clojure.org/datatypes.

The render function must return an Om/React component or something React knows how to render — such as a DOM representation of the component. The arguments to contacts-app are straightforward: data is the component state and owner is the backing React component.

Moving down the source file, in the implementation of render, we have the following:

```
(let [[selected-id :as selected-id-cursor]
      (:selected-contact-id data)]
  ...)
```

If we recall from our application state, the value of :selected-contact-id is, at this stage, an empty vector. Here, then, we are destructuring this vector and giving it a name. What you might be wondering now is why we bound the vector to a variable named selected-id-cursor. This is to reflect the fact that at this point in the life cycle of a component, selected-id-cursor isn't a vector any longer but rather it is a cursor.

Om cursors

Once `om/root` creates our root component, sub-components don't have direct access to the state atom any longer. Instead, components receive a cursor created from the application state.

Cursors are data structures that represent a place in the original state atom. You can use cursors to read, delete, update, or create a value with no knowledge of the original data structure. Let's take the `selected-id-cursor` cursor as an example:

```
{:contacts {1 {:id      1
               :name    "James Hetfield"
               :email   "james@metallica.com"
               :phone   "+1 XXX XXX XXX"}
            2 {:id      2
               :name    "Adam Darski"
               :email   "the.nergal@behemoth.pl"
               :phone   "+48 XXX XXX XXX"}}
 :selected-contact-id []
 :editing [false]}


                    ↑


        (:selected-contact-id app-state)


                    ↓


                cursor:
                  []
```

At the top, we have our original application state, which Om turns into a cursor. When we request the `:selected-contact-id` key from it, Om gives us another cursor representing that particular place in the data structure. It just so happens that its value is the empty vector.

What is interesting about this cursor is that if we update its value using one of Om's state transition functions such as `om/transact!` and `om/update!` — we will explain these shortly — it knows how to propagate the change up the tree and all the way back to the application state atom.

This is important because as we have briefly stated before, it is common practice to have our more specialized components depend on specific parts of the application state required for its correct operation.

By using cursors, we can easily propagate changes without knowing what the application state looks like, thus avoiding the need to access the global state.

> You can think of cursors as zippers. Conceptually, they serve a similar purpose but have different APIs.

Filling in the blanks

Moving down the contacts-app component, we now have the following:

```
(dom/div nil
            (om/build contacts-view
                    {:contacts              (:contacts data)
                     :selected-id-cursor selected-id-cursor})
            (om/build details-panel-view
                    {:contact        (get-in data [:contacts
selected-id])
                     :editing-cursor (:editing data)}))
```

The dom namespace contains thin wrappers around React's DOM classes. It's essentially the data structure representing what the application will look like. Next, we see two examples of how we can create Om components inside another Om component. We use the om/build function for that and create the contacts-view and details-panel-view components. The om/build function takes as arguments the component function, the component state, and, optionally, a map of options which aren't important for this example.

At this point, we have already started to limit the state we will pass into the sub-components by creating sub-cursors.

According to the source code, the next component we should look at is contacts-view. Here it is in full:

```
(defn contacts-view [{:keys [contacts selected-id-cursor]} owner]
  (reify
    om/IRender
    (render [_]
      (dom/div #js {:style #js {:float "left"
                                          :width "50%"}}
              (apply dom/ul nil
                    (om/build-all contact-summary-view (vals
contacts)
                                    {:shared {:selected-id-cursor
selected-id-cursor}})))))))
```

Hopefully, the source of this component looks a little more familiar now. As before, we reify om/IRender to provide a DOM representation of our component. It comprises a single div element. This time we give as the second argument to dom/div a hash-map representing HTML attributes. We are using some inline styles, but ideally we would use an external style sheet.

If you are not familiar with the #js {...} syntax, it's simply a reader macro that expands to (clj->js {...}) in order to convert a ClojureScript hash-map into a JavaScript object. The only thing to watch for is that it is not recursive, as evidenced by the nested use of #js.

The third argument to dom/div is slightly more complex than what we have seen so far:

```
(apply dom/ul nil
                      (om/build-all contact-summary-view (vals
contacts)
                                      {:shared {:selected-id-cursor
selected-id-cursor}}))
```

Each contact will be represented by a li (list item) HTML node, so we start by wrapping the result into a dom/ul element. Then, we use om/build-all to build a list of contact-summary-view components. Om will, in turn, call om/build for each contact in vals contacts.

Lastly, we use the third argument to om/build-all — the options map — to demonstrate how we can share state between components without the use of global state. We'll see how that's used in the next component, contact-summary-view:

```
(defn contact-summary-view [{:keys [name phone] :as contact} owner]
(reify
  om/IRender
  (render [_]
    (dom/li #js {:onClick #(select-contact! @contact
                                  (om/get-shared owner
:selected-id-cursor))}
            (dom/span nil name)
            (dom/span nil phone)))))
```

If we think of our application as a tree of components, we have now reached one of its leaves. This component simply returns a dom/li node with the contact's name and phone in it, wrapped in dom/span nodes.

It also installs a handler to the dom/li onClick event, which we can use to update the state cursor.

We use `om/get-shared` to access the shared state we installed earlier and pass the resulting cursor into `select-contact!` We also pass the current contact, but, if you look closely, we have to `deref` it first:

```
@contact
```

The reason for this is that Om doesn't allow us to manipulate cursors outside of the render phase. By derefing the cursor, we have its most recent underlying value. Now `select-contact!` has all it needs to perform the update:

```
(defn select-contact! [contact selected-id-cursor]
  (om/update! selected-id-cursor 0 (:id contact)))
```

We simply use `om/update!` to set the value of the `selected-id-cursor` cursor at index 0 to the `id` of the contact. As mentioned previously, the cursor takes care of propagating the change.

 You can think of `om/update!` as the cursors version of `clojure.core/reset!` used in atoms. Conversely, the same applies to `om/transact!` and `clojure.core/swap!`, respectively.

We are moving at a good pace. It's time we look at the next component, `details-panel-view`:

```
(defn details-panel-view [data owner]
  (reify
    om/IRender
    (render [_]
      (dom/div #js {:style #js {:float "right"
                                :width "50%"}}
               (om/build contact-details-view data)
               (om/build contact-details-form-view data)))))
```

This component should now look fairly familiar. All it does is build two other components, `contact-details-view` and `contact-details-form-view`:

```
(defn contact-details-view [{{:keys [name phone email id] :as contact}
                             :contact
                             editing :editing-cursor}
                            owner]
  (reify
    om/IRender
    (render [_]
      (dom/div #js {:style #js {:display (if (get editing 0) "none"
""}})
```

```
                     (dom/h2 nil "Contact details")
                     (if contact
                       (dom/div nil
                               (dom/h3 #js {:style #js {:margin-bottom
"0px"}} (:name contact))
                               (dom/span nil (:phone contact)) (dom/br nil)
                               (dom/span nil (:email contact)) (dom/br nil)
                               (dom/button #js {:onClick #(om/update! editing
0 true)}
                                         "Edit"))
                       (dom/span nil "No contact selected")))))))
```

The `contact-details-view` component receives two pieces of state: the contact and the editing flag. If we have a contact, we simply render the component. However, we use the editing flag to hide it, if we are editing it. This is so that we can show the edit form in the next component. We also install an `onClick` handler to the Edit button so that we can update the editing cursor.

The `contact-details-form-view` component receives the same arguments but renders the following form instead:

```
(defn contact-details-form-view [{{:keys [name phone email id] :as
contact} :contact
                                 editing :editing-cursor}
                                owner]
   (reify
     om/IRender
     (render [_]
       (dom/div #js {:style #js {:display (if (get editing 0) ""
"none")}}
               (dom/h2 nil "Contact details")
               (if contact
                 (dom/div nil
                         (dom/input #js {:type "text"
                                       :value name
                                       :onChange #(update-
contact! % contact :name)})
                         (dom/input #js {:type "text"
                                       :value phone
                                       :onChange #(update-
contact! % contact :phone)})
                         (dom/input #js {:type "text"
                                       :value email
                                       :onChange #(update-
contact! % contact :email)})
```

```
                                    (dom/button #js {:onClick #(om/update!
   editing 0 false)}
                                                        "Save"))
        (dom/div nil "No contact selected"))))))
```

This is the component responsible for actually updating the contact information based on the form. It does so by calling `update-contact!` with the JavaScript event, the contact cursor, and the key representing the attribute to be updated:

```
(defn update-contact! [e contact key]
  (om/update! contact key (.. e -target -value)))
```

As before, we simply use `om/update!` instead of `om/transact!` as we are simply replacing the value of the cursor attribute with the current value of the form field which triggered the event `e`.

> If you're not familiar with the `..` syntax, it's simply a convenience macro for Java and JavaScript interoperability. The previous example expands to:
>
> ```
> (. (. e -target) -value)
> ```
>
> This and other interoperability operators are described in the Java Interop page of the Clojure website (see `http://clojure.org/java_interop`).

This is it. Make sure your code is still compiling—or if you haven't yet, start the auto-compilation by typing the following in the terminal:

```
lein cljsbuild auto
```

Then, open up `dev-resources/public/index.html` again in your browser and take our Contacts app for a spin! Note in particular how the application state is always in sync while you edit the contact attributes.

If there are any issues at this stage, make sure the `src/cljs/contacts/core.cljs` file matches the companion code for this book.

Intercomponent communication

In our previous example, the components we built communicated with each other exclusively through the application state, both for reading and transacting data. While this approach works, it is not always the best except for very simple use cases. In this section, we will learn an alternate way of performing this communication using `core.async` channels.

The application we will build is a super simple virtual agile board. If you've heard of it, it's similar to Trello (see `https://trello.com/`). If you haven't, fear not, it's essentially a task management web application in which you have cards that represent tasks and you move them between columns such as **Backlog**, **In Progress**, and **Done**.

By the end of this section, the application will look like the following:

Backlog	In Progress	Done
Expenses Submit last client's expense report	Groceries shopping Almond milk, mixed nuts, eggs...	

We'll limit ourselves to a single feature: moving cards between columns by dragging and dropping them. Let's get started.

Creating an agile board with Om

We're already familiar with the `om-start` (see `https://github.com/magomimmo/om-start-template`) leiningen template, and since there is no reason to change it, that's what we will use to create our project—which I called `om-pm` for **Om Project Management**:

```
lein new om-start om-pm
cd om-pm
```

As before, we should ensure we have the right dependencies in our `project.clj` file:

```
:dependencies [[org.clojure/clojure "1.6.0"]
               [org.clojure/clojurescript "0.0-2511"]
               [org.om/om "0.8.1"]
               [org.clojure/core.async "0.1.346.0-17112a-alpha"]
               [com.facebook/react "0.12.2"]]
```

Now validate that we are in good shape by making sure the project compiles properly:

```
lein cljsbuild auto
Compiling ClojureScript.
Compiling "dev-resources/public/js/om_pm.js" from ("src/cljs" "dev-
resources/tools/repl")...
Successfully compiled "dev-resources/public/js/om_pm.js" in 13.101
seconds.
```

Next, open the `src/cljs/om_pm/core.cljs` file and add the namespaces that we will be using to build the application:

```
(ns om-pm.core
  (:require [om.core :as om :include-macros true]
            [om.dom :as dom :include-macros true]
            [cljs.core.async :refer [put! chan <!]]
            [om-pm.util :refer [set-transfer-data! get-transfer-data!
move-card!]])
  (:require-macros [cljs.core.async.macros :refer [go go-loop]]))
```

The main difference this time is that we are requiring `core.async` functions and macros. We don't yet have an `om-pm.util` namespace, but we'll get to that at the end.

The board state

It's time we think what our application state will look like. Our main entity in this application is the **card**, which represents a task and has the attributes `id`, `title`, and `description`. We will start by defining a couple of cards:

```
(def cards [{:id 1
             :title "Groceries shopping"
             :description "Almond milk, mixed nuts, eggs..."}
            {:id 2
             :title "Expenses"
             :description "Submit last client's expense report"}])
```

This isn't our application state yet, but rather a part of it. Another important piece of state is a way to track which cards are on which columns. To keep things simple, we will work with only three columns: **Backlog**, **In Progress**, and **Done**. By default, all cards start out in the backlog:

```
(def app-state
  (atom {:cards cards
         :columns [{:title "Backlog"
                    :cards (mapv :id cards)}
                   {:title "In Progress"
```

```
    :cards []}
  {:title "Done"
   :cards []}]}))
```

This is all the state we need. Columns have a `:title` and a `:cards` attribute, which contains the IDs of all cards in that column.

Additionally, we will have a helper function to make finding cards more convenient:

```
(defn card-by-id [id]
  (first (filterv #(= id (:id %)) cards)))
```

Beware of lazy sequences

You might have noticed the use of mapv instead of map for retrieving the cards IDs. This is a subtle but important difference: map is lazy by default, but Om can only create cursors for maps and vectors. Using mapv gives us a vector back, avoiding laziness altogether.

Had we not done that, Om would consider the list of IDs as a normal value and we would not be able to transact it.

Components overview

There are many ways to slice up an Om application into components, and in this section, we will present one way as we walk through each component's implementation.

The approach we will follow is similar to our previous application in that from this point on, we present the components bottom-up.

Before we see our first component, however, we should start with Om's own root component:

```
(om/root project-view app-state
         {:target (. js/document (getElementById "app"))})
```

This gives us a hint as to what our next component will be, project-view:

```
(defn project-view [app owner]
  (reify
    om/IInitState
    (init-state [_]
      {:transfer-chan (chan)})

    om/IWillMount
    (will-mount [_]
```

```
(let [transfer-chan (om/get-state owner :transfer-chan)]
  (go-loop []
    (let [transfer-data (<! transfer-chan)]
      (om/transact! app :columns
                    #(move-card! % transfer-data))
      (recur)))))

om/IRenderState
(render-state [this state]
  (dom/div nil
           (apply dom/ul nil
                  (om/build-all column-view (:columns app)
                                {:shared    {:cards (:cards app)}
                                 :init-state state}))))))
```

Lifecycle and component local state

The previous component is fairly different from the ones we have seen so far. More specifically, it implements two new protocols: om/IInitState and om/IWillMount. Additionally, we dropped om/IRender altogether in favor of om/IRenderState. Before we explain what these new protocols are good for, we need to discuss our high-level design.

The project-view component is our application's main entry point and receives the whole application state as its first argument. As in our earlier *Contacts* application, it then instantiates the remaining components with the data they need.

Different from the *Contacts* example, however, it creates a core.async channel—transfer-chan—which works as a message bus. The idea is that when we drag a card from one column and drop it on another, one of our components will put a transfer event in this channel and let someone else—most likely a go block—perform the actual move operation.

This is done in the following snippet taken from the component shown earlier:

```
om/IInitState
(init-state [_]
  {:transfer-chan (chan)})
```

This creates what Om calls the component local state. It uses a different lifecycle protocol, om/IInitState, which is guaranteed to be called only once. After all, we need a single channel for this component. init-state should return a map representing the local state.

Now that we have the channel, we need to install a `go-loop` to handle messages sent to it. For this purpose, we use a different protocol:

```
om/IWillMount
(will-mount [_]
  (let [transfer-chan (om/get-state owner :transfer-chan)]
    (go-loop []
      (let [transfer-data (<! transfer-chan)]
        (om/transact! app :columns #(move-card! % transfer-data))
        (recur)))))
```

Like the previous protocol, `om/IWillMount` is also guaranteed to be called once in the component life cycle. It is called when it is about to be mounted into the DOM and is the perfect place to install the `go-loop` into our channel.

When creating `core.async` channels in Om applications, it is important to avoid creating them inside life-cycle functions that are called multiple times. Besides non-deterministic behavior, this is a source of memory leaks.

We get hold of it from the component local state using the `om/get-state` function. Once we get a message, we transact the state. We will see what `transfer-data` looks like very shortly.

We complete the component by implementing its render function:

```
. . .
om/IRenderState
    (render-state [this state]
      (dom/div nil
              (apply dom/ul nil
                    (om/build-all column-view (:columns app)
                                    {:shared     {:cards (:cards app)}
                                     :init-state state})))))
. . .
```

The `om/IRenderState` function serves the same purpose of `om/IRender`, that is, it should return the DOM representation of what the component should look like. However, it defines a different function, `render-state`, which receives the component local state as its second argument. This state contains the map we created during the `init-state` phase.

Remaining components

Next, we will build multiple `column-view` components, one per column. Each of them receives the list of cards from the application state as their shared state. We will use that to retrieve the card details from the IDs we store in each column.

We also use the `:init-state` key to initialize the local state of each column view with our channel, since all columns need a reference to it. Here's what the component looks like:

```
(defn column-view [{:keys [title cards]} owner]
  (reify
    om/IRenderState
    (render-state [this {:keys [transfer-chan]}]
      (dom/div #js {:style      #js {:border  "1px solid black"
                                     :float   "left"
                                     :height  "100%"
                                     :width   "320px"
                                     :padding "10px"}
                    :onDragOver #(.preventDefault %)
                    :onDrop     #(handle-drop % transfer-chan title)}
        (dom/h2 nil title)
        (apply dom/ul #js {:style #js {:list-style-type "none"
                                       :padding         "0px"}}
          (om/build-all (partial card-view title)
                        (mapv card-by-id cards)))))))
```

The code should look fairly familiar at this point. We used inline CSS in the example to keep it simple, but in a real application, we would probably have used an external style sheet.

We implement `render-state` once more to retrieve the transfer channel, which will be used when handling the `onDrop` JavaScript event. This event is fired by the browser when a user drops a draggable DOM element onto this component. `handle-drop` takes care of that like so:

```
(defn handle-drop [e transfer-chan column-title]
  (.preventDefault e)
  (let [data {:card-id
              (js/parseInt (get-transfer-data! e "cardId"))
              :source-column
              (get-transfer-data! e "sourceColumn")
              :destination-column
              column-title}]
    (put! transfer-chan data)))
```

This function creates the transfer data—a map with the keys `:card-id`, `:source-column`, and `:destination-column`—which is everything we need to move the cards between columns. Finally, we `put!` it into the transfer channel.

Next, we build a number or `card-view` components. As mentioned previously, Om can't create cursors from lazy sequences, so we use `filterv` to give each `card-view` a vector containing their respective cards. Let's see its source:

```
(defn card-view [column {:keys [id title description] :as card} owner]
  (reify
    om/IRender
    (render [this]
      (dom/li #js {:style #js {:border "1px solid black"}
                   :draggable true
                   :onDragStart (fn [e]
                                  (set-transfer-data! e "cardId" id)
                                  (set-transfer-data! e "sourceColumn"
column))}
              (dom/span nil title)
              (dom/p nil description)))))
```

As this component doesn't need any local state, we go back to using the `IRender` protocol. Additionally, we make it draggable and install an event handler on the `onDragStart` event, which will be triggered when the user starts dragging the card.

This event handler sets the transfer data, which we use from `handle-drop`.

We have glossed over the fact that these components use a few utility functions. That's OK, as we will now define them in a new namespace.

Utility functions

Go ahead and create a new file under `src/cljs/om_pm/` called `util.cljs` and add the following namespace declaration:

```
(ns om-pm.util)
```

For consistency, we will look at the functions bottom-up, starting with `move-card!`:

```
(defn column-idx [title columns]
  (first (keep-indexed (fn [idx column]
                         (when (= title (:title column))
                           idx))
                       columns)))
```

```
(defn move-card! [columns {:keys [card-id source-column destination-
column]}]
   (let [from (column-idx source-column      columns)
         to   (column-idx destination-column columns)]
    (-> columns
        (update-in [from :cards] (fn [cards]
                                   (remove #{card-id} cards)))
        (update-in [to   :cards] (fn [cards]
                                   (conj cards card-id)))))))
```

The move-card! function receives a cursor for the columns in our application state and simply moves card-id between the source and destination. You will notice we didn't need any access to core.async or Om specific functions, which means this function is pure and therefore easy to test.

Next, we have the functions that handle transfer data:

```
(defn set-transfer-data! [e key value]
   (.setData (-> e .-nativeEvent .-dataTransfer)
             key value))

(defn get-transfer-data! [e key]
   (-> (-> e .-nativeEvent .-dataTransfer)
       (.getData key)))
```

These functions use JavaScript interoperability to interact with HTML's DataTransfer (see https://developer.mozilla.org/en-US/docs/Web/API/DataTransfer) object. This is how browsers share data related to drag and drop events.

Now, let's simply save the file and make sure the code compiles properly. We can finally open dev-resources/public/index.html in the browser and play around with the product of our work!

Exercises

In this exercise, we will modify the om-pm project we created in the previous section. The objective is to add keyboard shortcuts so that power users can operate the agile board more efficiently.

The shortcuts to be supported are:

- The up, down, left, and right arrow keys: These allow the user to navigate through the cards, highlighting the current one
- The n and p keys: These are used to move the current card to the next (right) or previous (left) column, respectively

The key insight here is to create a new `core.async` channel, which will contain key press events. These events will then trigger the actions outlined previously. We can use the Google closure library to listen for events. Just add the following `require` to the application namespace:

```
(:require [goog.events :as events])
```

Then, use this function to create a channel from DOM events:

```
(defn listen [el type]
  (let [c (chan)]
    (events/listen el type #(put! c %))
    c))
```

The actual logic of moving the cards around based on keyboard shortcuts can be implemented in a number of ways, so don't forget to compare your solution with the answers provided in this book's companion code.

Summary

In this chapter, we saw a different approach on how to handle reactive web interfaces by Om and React. In turn, these frameworks make this possible and painless by applying functional programming principles such as immutability and persistent data structures for efficient rendering.

We also learned to think the Om way by structuring our applications as a series of functions, which receive state and output a DOM representation of state changes.

Additionally, we saw that by structuring application state transitions through `core.async` channels, we separate the presentation logic from the code, which will actually perform the work, making our components even easier to reason about.

In the next chapter, we will turn to an often overlooked yet useful tool for creating reactive applications: **Futures**.

8
Futures

The first step towards reactive applications is to break out of synchronous processing. In general, applications waste a lot of time waiting for things to happen. Maybe we are waiting on an expensive computation—say, calculating the 1000th Fibonacci number. Perhaps we are waiting for some information to be written to the database. We could also be waiting for a network call to return, bringing us the latest recommendations from our favorite online store.

Regardless of what we're waiting for, we should never block clients of our application. This is crucial to achieve the responsiveness we desire when building reactive systems.

In an age where processing cores are abundant—my MacBook Pro has eight processor cores—blocking APIs severely underutilizes the resources we have at our disposal.

As we approach the end of this book, it is appropriate to step back a little and appreciate that not all classes of problems that deal with concurrent, asynchronous computations require the machinery of frameworks such as RxJava or `core.async`.

In this chapter, we will look at another abstraction that helps us develop concurrent, asynchronous applications: **futures**. We will learn about:

- The problems and limitations with Clojure's implementation of futures
- An alternative to Clojure's futures that provides asynchronous, composable semantics
- How to optimize concurrency in the face of blocking IO

Clojure futures

The first step toward fixing this issue — that is, to prevent a potentially long-running task from blocking our application — is to create new threads, which do the work and wait for it to complete. This way, we keep the application's main thread free to serve more clients.

Working directly with threads, however, is tedious and error-prone, so Clojure's core library includes futures, which are extremely simple to use:

```
(def f (clojure.core/future
          (println "doing some expensive work...")
          (Thread/sleep 5000)
          (println "done")
          10))
(println "You'll see me before the future finishes")
;; doing some expensive work...
;; You'll see me before the future finishes
;; done
```

In the preceding snippet, we invoke the `clojure.core/future` macro with a body simulating an expensive computation. In this example, it simply sleeps for 5 seconds before returning the value 10. As the output demonstrates, this does not block the main thread, which is free to serve more clients, pick work items from a queue, or what have you.

Of course, the most interesting computations, such as the expensive one, return results we care about. This is where the first limitation of Clojure futures becomes apparent. If we attempt to retrieve the result of a future — by derefing it — before it has completed, the calling thread will block until the future returns a value. Try running the following slightly modified version of the previous snippet:

```
(def f (clojure.core/future
          (println "doing some expensive work...")
          (Thread/sleep 5000)
          (println "done")
          10))
(println "You'll see me before the future finishes")
@f
(println "I could be doing something else. Instead I had to wait")


;; doing some expensive work...
;; You'll see me before the future finishes
;; 5 SECONDS LATER
;; done
;; I could be doing something else. Instead, I had to wait
```

The only difference now is that we immediately try to *deref* the future after we create it. Since the future isn't done, we sit there waiting for 5 seconds until it returns its value. Only then is our program allowed to continue.

In general, this poses a problem when building modular systems. Often, a long-running operation like the one described earlier would be initiated within a specific module or function, and handed over to the next logical step for further processing.

Clojure futures don't allow us to schedule a function to be executed when the future finishes in order to perform such further processing. This is an important feature in building reactive systems.

Fetching data in parallel

To understand better the issues outlined in the previous section, let's build a more complex example that fetches data about one of my favorite movies, *The Lord of the Rings*.

The idea is that given the movie, we wish to retrieve its actors and, for each actor, retrieve the movies they have been a part of. We also would like to find out more information about each actor, such as their spouses.

Additionally, we will match each actor's movie against the list of top five movies in order to highlight them as such. Finally, the result will be printed to the screen.

From the problem statement, we identify the following two main characteristics we will need to account for:

- Some of these tasks need to be performed in parallel
- They establish dependencies on each other

To get started, let's create a new leiningen project:

```
lein new clj-futures-playground
```

Next, open the core namespace file in `src/clj_futures_playground/core.clj` and add the data we will be working with:

```
(ns clj-futures-playground.core
  (:require [clojure.pprint :refer [pprint]]))

(def movie
  {:name "Lord of The Rings: The Fellowship of The Ring"
   :cast ["Cate Blanchett"
          "Elijah Wood"
```

```
          "Liv Tyler"
          "Orlando Bloom"]})

(def actor-movies
  [{:name "Cate Blanchett"
    :movies ["Lord of The Rings: The Fellowship of The Ring"
             "Lord of The Rings: The Return of The King"
             "The Curious Case of Benjamin Button"]}

   {:name "Elijah Wood"
    :movies ["Eternal Sunshine of the Spotless Mind"
             "Green Street Hooligans"
             "The Hobbit: An Unexpected Journey"]}

   {:name "Liv Tyler"
    :movies ["Lord of The Rings: The Fellowship of The Ring"
             "Lord of The Rings: The Return of The King"
             "Armageddon"]}

   {:name "Orlando Bloom"
    :movies ["Lord of The Rings: The Fellowship of The Ring"
             "Lord of The Rings: The Return of The King"
             "Pirates of the Caribbean: The Curse of the Black
Pearl"]}])

(def actor-spouse
  [{:name "Cate Blanchett"      :spouse "Andrew Upton"}
   {:name "Elijah Wood"         :spouse "Unknown"}
   {:name "Liv Tyler"           :spouse "Royston Langdon"}
   {:name "Orlando Bloom"       :spouse "Miranda Kerr"}])
(def top-5-movies
  ["Lord of The Rings: The Fellowship of The Ring"
   "The Matrix"
   "The Matrix Reloaded"
   "Pirates of the Caribbean: The Curse of the Black Pearl"
   "Terminator"])
```

The namespace declaration is simple and only requires the pprint function, which will help us print our result in an easy-to-read format. With all the data in place, we can create the functions that will simulate remote services responsible for fetching the relevant data:

```
(defn cast-by-movie [name]
  (future (do (Thread/sleep 5000)
              (:cast movie))))
```

```
(defn movies-by-actor [name]
  (do (Thread/sleep 2000)
      (->> actor-movies
           (filter #(= name (:name %)))
           first)))

(defn spouse-of [name]
  (do (Thread/sleep 2000)
      (->> actor-spouse
           (filter #(= name (:name %)))
           first)))

(defn top-5 []
  (future (do (Thread/sleep 5000)
              top-5-movies)))
```

Each `service` function sleeps the current thread by a given amount of time to simulate a slow network. The functions `cast-by-movie` and `Top 5` each returns a future, indicating we wish to fetch this data on a different thread. The remaining functions simply return the actual data. They will also be executed in a different thread, however, as we will see shortly.

The next thing we need is a function to aggregate all fetched data, match spouses to actors, and highlight movies in the **Top 5** list. We'll call it the `aggregate-actor-data` function:

```
(defn aggregate-actor-data [spouses movies top-5]
  (map (fn [{:keys [name spouse]} {:keys [movies]}]
         {:name    name
          :spouse spouse
          :movies (map (fn [m]
                         (if (some #{m} top-5)
                           (str m " - (top 5)")
                           m))
                       movies)})
       spouses
       movies))
```

The preceding function is fairly straightforward. It simply zips spouses and movies together, building a map of keys :name, :spouse, and :movies. It further transforms `movies` to append the **Top 5** suffix to the ones in the `top-5` list.

The last piece of the puzzle is the `-main` function, which allows us to run the program from the command line:

```
(defn -main [& args]
  (time (let [cast    (cast-by-movie "Lord of The Rings: The
Fellowship of The Ring")
              movies  (pmap movies-by-actor @cast)
              spouses (pmap spouse-of @cast)
              top-5   (top-5)]
          (prn "Fetching data...")
          (pprint (aggregate-actor-data spouses movies @top-5))
          (shutdown-agents))))
```

There are a number of things worth highlighting in the preceding snippet.

First, we wrap the whole body in a call to `time`, a simple benchmarking function that comes with Clojure. This is just so we know how long the program took to fetch all data — this information will become relevant later.

Then, we set up a number of `let` bindings. The first, `cast`, is the result of calling `cast-by-movie`, which returns a future.

The next binding, `movies`, uses a function we haven't seen before: `pmap`.

The `pmap` function works like `map`, except the function is mapped over the items in the list in parallel. The `pmap` function uses futures under the covers and that is the reason `movies-by-actor` doesn't return a future — it leaves that for `pmap` to handle.

> The pmap function is actually meant for CPU-bound operations, but is used here to keep the code simple. In the face of blocking IO, pmap wouldn't perform optimally. We will talk more about blocking IO later in this chapter.

We get the list of actors by *derefing* the `cast` binding, which, as we saw in the previous section, blocks the current thread waiting for the asynchronous fetch to finish. Once all results are ready, we simply call the `aggregate-actor-data` function.

Lastly, we call the `shutdown-agents` function, which shuts down the **Thread Pool** backing futures in Clojure. This is necessary for our program to terminate properly, otherwise it would simply hang in the terminal.

To run the program, type the following in the terminal, under the project's root directory:

```
lein run -m clj-futures-playground.core
```

```
"Fetching data..."
({:name "Cate Blanchett",
  :spouse "Andrew Upton",
  :movies
  ("Lord of The Rings: The Fellowship of The Ring - (top 5)"
   "Lord of The Rings: The Return of The King"
   "The Curious Case of Benjamin Button")}
 {:name "Elijah Wood",
  :spouse "Unknown",
  :movies
  ("Eternal Sunshine of the Spotless Mind"
   "Green Street Hooligans"
   "The Hobbit: An Unexpected Journey")}
 {:name "Liv Tyler",
  :spouse "Royston Langdon",
  :movies
  ("Lord of The Rings: The Fellowship of The Ring - (top 5)"
   "Lord of The Rings: The Return of The King"
   "Armageddon")}
 {:name "Orlando Bloom",
  :spouse "Miranda Kerr",
  :movies
  ("Lord of The Rings: The Fellowship of The Ring - (top 5)"
   "Lord of The Rings: The Return of The King"
   "Pirates of the Caribbean: The Curse of the Black Pearl - (top 5)")})
"Elapsed time: 10120.267 msecs"
```

You will have noticed that the program takes a while to print the first message. Additionally, because futures block when they are derefed , the program doesn't start fetching the list of top five movies until it has completely finished fetching the cast of *The Lord of The Rings*.

Let's have a look at why that is so:

```
(time (let [cast    (cast-by-movie "Lord of The Rings: The
Fellowship of The Ring")
            ;; the following line blocks
            movies  (pmap movies-by-actor @cast)
            spouses (pmap spouse-of @cast)
            top-5   (top-5)]
```

The highlighted section in the preceding snippet shows where the program blocks waiting for `cast-by-movie` to finish. As stated previously, Clojure futures don't give us a way to run some piece of code when the future finishes — like a callback — forcing us to block too soon.

This prevents `top-5` — a completely independent parallel data fetch — from running before we retrieve the movie's cast.

Of course, this is a contrived example, and we could solve this particular annoyance by calling `top-5` before anything else. The problem is that the solution isn't always crystal clear and ideally we should not have to worry about the order of execution.

As we will see in the next section, there is a better way.

Imminent – a composable futures library for Clojure

In the past few months, I have been working on an open source library that aims to fix the previous issues with Clojure futures. The result of this work is called *imminent* (see `https://github.com/leonardoborges/imminent`).

The fundamental difference is that imminent futures are asynchronous by default and provide a number of combinators that allow us to declaratively write our programs without having to worry about its order of execution.

The best way to demonstrate how the library works is to rewrite the previous movies example in it. We will do this in two steps.

First, we will examine individually the bits of imminent's API that will be part of our final solution. Then, we'll put it all together in a working application. Let's start by creating a new project:

```
lein new imminent-playground
```

Next, add a dependency on imminent to your `project.clj`:

```
:dependencies [[org.clojure/clojure "1.6.0"]
               [com.leonardoborges/imminent "0.1.0"]]
```

Then, create a new file, `src/imminent_playground/repl.clj`, and add imminent's core namespace:

```
(ns imminent-playground.repl
  (:require [imminent.core :as Ii]))
```

```
(def  repl-out *out*)
(defn prn-to-repl [& args]
  (binding [*out* repl-out]
    (apply prn args)))
```

The preceding snippet also creates a helper function that is useful when we're dealing with multiple threads in the REPL—this will be explained in detail later, but for now just take this as being a reliable way to print to the REPL across multiple threads.

Feel free to type this in the REPL as we go along. Otherwise, you can require the namespace file from a running REPL like so:

```
(require 'imminent-playground.repl)
```

All the following examples should be in this file.

Creating futures

Creating a future in imminent isn't much different from creating a future in Clojure. It's as simple as the following:

```
(def age (i/future 31))

;; #<Future@2ea0ca7d: #<Success@3e4dec75: 31>>
```

What looks very different, however, is the return value. A key decision in imminent's API is to represent the value of a computation as either a Success or a Failure type. Success, as in the preceding example, wraps the result of the computation. Failure, as you might have guessed, will wrap any exceptions that happened in the future:

```
(def failed-computation  (i/future (throw (Exception. "Error"))))
;; #<Future@63cd0d58: #<Failure@2b273f98: #<Exception java.lang.
Exception: Error>>>

(def failed-computation-1 (i/failed-future :invalid-data))
;; #<Future@a03588f: #<Failure@61ab196b: :invalid-data>>
```

As you can see, you're not limited to exceptions only. We can use the failed-future function to create a future that completes immediately with the given reason, which, in the second example, is simply a keyword.

The next question we might ask is "How do we get the result out of a future?". As with Clojure futures, we can deref it as follows:

```
@age          ;; #<Success@3e4dec75: 31>
(deref @age)  ;; 31
(i/dderef age) ;; 31
```

The idiom of using a double-deref is common, so imminent provides the convenience shown, `dderef`, which is equivalent to calling `deref` twice.

However, different from Clojure futures, this is a non-blocking operation, so if the future hasn't completed yet, the following is what you'll get:

```
@(i/future (do (Thread/sleep 500)
               "hello"))
;; :imminent.future/unresolved
```

The initial state of a future is `unresolved`, so unless you are absolutely certain a future has completed, derefing might not be the best way to work with the result of a computation. This is where combinators become useful.

Combinators and event handlers

Let's say we would like to double the value in the age future. As we would with lists, we can simply map a function over the future to do just this:

```
(def double-age (i/map age #(* % 2)))
;; #<Future@659684cb: #<Success@7ce85f87: 62>>
```

 While `i/future` schedules its body for execution on a separate thread, it's worth noting that future combinators such as `map`, `filter`, and so on, do not create a new thread immediately. Instead, they schedule a function to be executed asynchronously in the thread pool once the original future completes.

Another way to do something with the value of a future is to use the `on-success` event handler that gets called with the wrapped value of the future in case it is successful:

```
(i/on-success age #(prn-to-repl (str "Age is: " %)))
;; "Age is: 31"
```

Similarly, an `on-failure` handler exists, which does the same for `Failure` types. While on the subject of failures, imminent futures understand the context in which they are being executed and, if the current future yields a `Failure`, it simply short-circuits the computation:

```
(-> failed-computation
    (i/map #(* % 2)))
;; #<Future@7f74297a: #<Failure@2b273f98: #<Exception java.lang.
Exception: Error>>>
```

In the preceding example, we don't get a new error, but rather the original exception contained in `failed-computation`. The function passed to `map` never runs.

The decision to wrap the result of a future in a type such as `Success` or `Failure` might seem arbitrary but is actually quite the opposite. Both types implement the protocol `IReturn` — and a couple of other ones — which comes with a set of useful functions, one of which is `map`:

```
(i/map (i/success "hello")
       #(str % " world"))
;; #<Success@714eea92: "hello world">

(i/map (i/failure "error")
       #(str % " world"))
;; #<Failure@6d685b65: "error">
```

We get a similar behavior here as we did previously: mapping a function over a failure simply short-circuits the whole computation. If you do, however, wish to map over the failure, you can use map's counterpart map-failure, which behaves similarly to map but is its inverse:

```
(i/map-failure (i/success "hello")
               #(str % " world"))
;; #<Success@779af3f4: "hello">

(i/map-failure (i/failure "Error")
               #(str "We failed: " %))
;; #<Failure@52a02597: "We failed: Error">
```

This plays well with the last event handlers imminent provides — on-complete:

```
(i/on-complete age
               (fn [result]
                 (i/map result #(prn-to-repl "success: " %))
                 (i/map-failure result #(prn-to-repl "error: " %))))

;; "success: " 31
```

On contrary to on-success and on-failure, on-complete calls the provided function with the result type wrapper, so it is a convenient way to handle both cases in a single function.

Coming back to combinators, sometimes we will need to map a function over a future, which itself returns a future:

```
(defn range-future [n]
  (i/const-future (range n)))

(def age-range (i/map age range-future))

;; #<Future@3d24069e: #<Success@82e8e6e: #<Future@2888dbf4:
#<Success@312084f6: (0 1 2...)>>>>
```

The `range-future` function returns a successful future that yields a range of *n*. The `const-future` function is analogous to `failed-future`, except it immediately completes the future with a `Success` type.

However, we end up with a nested future, which is almost never what you want. That's OK. This is precisely the scenario in which you would use another combinator, `flatmap`.

You can think of it as `mapcat` for futures — it flattens the computation for us:

```
(def age-range (i/flatmap age range-future))

;; #<Future@601c1dfc: #<Success@55f4bcaf: (0 1 2 ...)>>
```

Another very useful combinator is used to bring together multiple computations to be used in a single function — `sequence`:

```
(def name (i/future (do (Thread/sleep 500)
                        "Leo")))
(def genres (i/future (do (Thread/sleep 500)
                          ["Heavy Metal" "Black Metal" "Death Metal"
"Rock 'n Roll"])))

(-> (i/sequence [name age genres])
    (i/on-success
     (fn [[name age genres]]
       (prn-to-repl (format "%s is %s years old and enjoys %s"
                            name
                            age
                            (clojure.string/join "," genres))))))

;; "Leo is 31 years old and enjoys Heavy Metal,Black Metal,Death
Metal,Rock 'n Roll"
```

Essentially, `sequence` creates a new future, which will complete only when all other futures in the vector have completed or any one of them have failed.

This is a nice segue into the last combinator we will look at—map-future—which we would use in place of pmap, used in the movies example:

```
(defn calculate-double [n]
  (i/const-future (* n 2)))

(-> (i/map-future calculate-double [1 2 3 4])
    i/await
    i/dderef)

;; [2 4 6 8]
```

In the preceding example, calculate-double is a function that returns a future with the value n doubled. The map-future function then maps calculate-double over the list, effectively performing the calculations in parallel. Finally, map-future sequences all futures together, returning a single future, which yields the result of all computations.

Because we are performing a number of parallel computations and don't really know when they will finish, we call await on the future, which is a way to block the current thread until its result is ready. In general, you would use the combinators and event handlers instead, but for this example, using await is acceptable.

Imminent's API provides many more combinators, which help us write asynchronous programs in a declarative way. This section gave us a taste of what is possible with the API and is enough to allow us to write the movies example using imminent futures.

The movies example revisited

Still within our imminent-playground project, open the src/imminent_playground/core.clj file and add the appropriate definitions:

```
(ns imminent-playground.core
  (:require [clojure.pprint :refer [pprint]]
            [imminent.core :as i]))

(def movie ...)

(def actor-movies ...)

(def actor-spouse ...)

(def top-5-movies ...)
```

We will be using the same data as in the previous program, represented in the preceding snippet by the use of ellipses. Simply copy the relevant declarations over.

The service functions will need small tweaks in this new version:

```
(defn cast-by-movie [name]
  (i/future (do (Thread/sleep 5000)
                (:cast  movie))))

(defn movies-by-actor [name]
  (i/future (do (Thread/sleep 2000)
                (->> actor-movies
                     (filter #(= name (:name %)))
                     first))))

(defn spouse-of [name]
  (i/future (do (Thread/sleep 2000)
                (->> actor-spouse
                     (filter #(= name (:name %)))
                     first))))

(defn top-5 []
  (i/future (do (Thread/sleep 5000)
                top-5-movies)))

(defn aggregate-actor-data [spouses movies top-5]
  ...)
```

The main difference is that all of them now return an imminent future. The `aggregate-actor-data` function is also the same as before.

This brings us to the `-main` function, which was rewritten to use imminent combinators:

```
(defn -main [& args]
  (time (let [cast     (cast-by-movie "Lord of The Rings: The
Fellowship of The Ring")
              movies   (i/flatmap cast #(i/map-future movies-by-actor
%))
              spouses  (i/flatmap cast #(i/map-future spouse-of %))
              result   (i/sequence [spouses movies (top-5)])]
          (prn "Fetching data...")
          (pprint (apply aggregate-actor-data
                         (i/dderef (i/await result)))))))
```

The function starts much like its previous version, and even the first binding, `cast`, looks familiar. Next we have `movies`, which is obtained by fetching an actor's movies in parallel. This in itself returns a future, so we `flatmap` it over the `cast` future to obtain our final result:

```
movies   (i/flatmap cast #(i/map-future movies-by-actor %))
```

`spouses` works in exactly the same way as `movies`, which brings us to `result`. This is where we would like to bring all asynchronous computations together. Therefore, we use the `sequence` combinator:

```
result   (i/sequence [spouses movies (top-5)])
```

Finally, we decide to block on the `result` future—by using await—so we can print the final result:

```
(pprint (apply aggregate-actor-data
                   (i/dderef (i/await result))))
```

We run the program in the same way as before, so simply type the following in the command line, under the project's root directory:

```
lein run -m imminent-playground.core
"Fetching data..."
({:name "Cate Blanchett",
  :spouse "Andrew Upton",
  :movies
  ("Lord of The Rings: The Fellowship of The Ring - (top 5)"
   "Lord of The Rings: The Return of The King"
   "The Curious Case of Benjamin Button")}
...
"Elapsed time: 7088.398 msecs"
```

The result output was trimmed as it is exactly the same as before, but two things are different and deserve attention:

- The first output, **Fetching data...**, is printed to the screen a lot faster than in the example using Clojure futures
- The overall time it took to fetch all that is shorter, clocking in at just over 7 seconds

This highlights the asynchronous nature of imminent futures and combinators. The only time we had to wait is when we explicitly called `await` at the end of the program.

More specifically, the performance boost comes from the following section in the code:

```
(let [...
      result  (i/sequence [spouses movies (top-5)])]
   ...)
```

Because none of the previous bindings block the current thread, we never have to wait to kick off `top-5` in parallel, shaving off roughly 3 seconds from the overall execution time. We didn't have to explicitly think about the order of execution — the combinators simply did the right thing.

Finally, one last difference is that we didn't have to explicitly call `shutdown-agents` as before. The reason for this is that imminent uses a different type of thread pool: a `ForkJoinPool` (see `http://docs.oracle.com/javase/7/docs/api/java/util/concurrent/ForkJoinPool.html`).

This pool has a number of advantages — each with its own trade-off — over the other thread pools, and one characteristic is that we don't need to explicitly shut it down — all threads it creates daemon threads.

When the JVM shuts down, it hangs waiting for all non-daemon threads to finish. Only then does it exit. That's why using Clojure futures would cause the JVM to hang, if we had not called `shutdown-agents`.

All threads created by the ForkJoinPool are set as daemon threads by default: when the JVM attempts to shut down, and if the only threads running are daemon ones, they are abandoned and the JVM exits gracefully.

Combinators such as `map` and `flatmap`, as well as the functions `sequence` and `map-future`, aren't exclusive to futures. They have many more fundamental principles by which they abide, making them useful in a range of domains. Understanding these principles isn't necessary for following the contents of this book. Should you want to know more about these principles, please refer to the *Appendix, The Algebra of Library Design*.

Futures and blocking IO

The choice of using ForkJoinPool for imminent is deliberate. The ForkJoinPool—added on Java 7—is extremely smart. When created, you give it a desired level of `parallelism`, which defaults to the number of available processors.

ForkJoinPool then attempts to honor the desired parallelism by dynamically shrinking and expanding the pool as required. When a task is submitted to this pool, it doesn't necessarily create a new thread if it doesn't have to. This allows the pool to serve an extremely large number of tasks with a much smaller number of actual threads.

However, it cannot guarantee such optimizations in the face of blocking IO, as it can't know whether the thread is blocking waiting for an external resource. Nevertheless, ForkJoinPool provides a mechanism by which threads can notify the pool when they might block.

Imminent takes advantage of this mechanism by implementing the `ManagedBlocker` (see `http://docs.oracle.com/javase/7/docs/api/java/util/concurrent/ForkJoinPool.ManagedBlocker.html`) interface—and provides another way to create futures, as demonstrated here:

```
(-> (immi/blocking-future
     (Thread/sleep 100)
     10)
    (immi/await))
;; #<Future@4c8ac77a: #<Success@45525276: 10>>

(-> (immi/blocking-future-call
     (fn []
       (Thread/sleep 100)
       10))
    (immi/await))
;; #<Future@37162438: #<Success@5a13697f: 10>>
```

The `blocking-future` and `blocking-future-call` have the same semantics as their counterparts, `future` and `future-call`, but should be used when the task to be performed is of a blocking nature (that is, not CPU-bound). This allows the ForkJoinPool to better utilize its resources, making it a powerful and flexible solution.

Summary

In this chapter, we learned that Clojure futures leave a lot to be desired. More specifically, Clojure futures don't provide a way to express dependencies between results. It doesn't mean, however, that we should dismiss futures altogether.

They are still a useful abstraction and with the right semantics for asynchronous computations and a rich set of combinators—such as the ones provided by imminent—they can be a big ally in building reactive applications that are performant and responsive. Sometimes, this is all we need.

For the times where we need to model data that varies over time, we turn to richer frameworks inspired by **Functional Reactive Programming (FRP)** and **Compositional Event Systems (CES)** —such as RxJava—or **Communicating Sequential Processes (CSP)** —such as core.async. As they have a lot more to offer, much of this book has been dedicated to those approaches.

In the next chapter, we will go back to discussing FRP/CES by way of a case study.

9
A Reactive API to Amazon Web Services

Throughout this book, we have learned a number of tools and techniques to aid us in building reactive applications—futures with imminent, Observables with RxClojure/RxJava, channels with `core.async`—and even in building reactive user interfaces using Om and React.

In the process, we also became acquainted with the concept of **Functional Reactive Programming** and **Compositional Event Systems**, as well as what makes them different.

In this last chapter, we will bring a few of these different tools and concepts together by developing an application based on a real-world use case from a client I worked with in Sydney, Australia. We will:

- Describe the problem of infrastructure automation we were trying to solve
- Have a brief look at some of Amazon's AWS services
- Build an AWS dashboard using the concepts we have learned so far

The problem

This client—which we will call BubbleCorp from now on—had a big problem that is all too common and well known to big enterprises: one massive monolithic application.

Besides making them move slow, as individual components can't be evolved independently, this application makes deployment incredibly hard due to its environment constraints: all infrastructure needs to be available in order for the application to work at all.

As a result, developing new features and bug fixes involves having only a handful of development environments shared across dozens of developers each. This requires a wasteful amount of coordination between teams just so that they won't step on each other's toes, contributing to slow the whole life-cycle further.

The long-term solution to this problem is to break down this big application into smaller components, which can be deployed and worked on independently, but as good as this sounds, it's a laborious and lengthy process.

As a first step, BubbleCorp decided the best thing they could improve in the short term is to give developers the ability to work in the application independently from each other, which implies being able to create a new environment as well.

Given the infrastructure constraints, running the application on a single developer machine is prohibitive.

Instead, they turned to infrastructure automation: they wanted a tool that, with the press of a button, would spin up a completely new environment.

This new environment would be already preconfigured with the proper application servers, database instances, DNS entries, and everything else needed to run the application.

This way, developers would only need to deploy their code and test their changes, without having to worry about the application setup.

Infrastructure automation

Amazon Web Services (**AWS**) is the most mature and comprehensive cloud computing platform available today, and as such it was a natural choice for BubbleCorp to host its infrastructure in.

If you haven't used AWS before, don't worry, we'll focus only on a few of its services:

- **Elastic Compute Cloud** (**EC2**): A service that provides users with the ability to rent virtual computers in which to run their applications.
- **Relational Database Service** (**RDS**): This can be thought of as a specialized version of EC2 that provides managed database services.
- **CloudFormation**: With CloudFormation, users have the ability to specify infrastructure templates, called stacks, of several different AWS resources — such as EC2, AWS, and many others — as well as how they interact with each other. Once written, the infrastructure template can be sent to AWS to be executed.

For **BubbleCorp**, the idea was to write these infrastructure templates, which once submitted would result into a completely new, isolated environment containing all data and components required to run its app. At any given time, there would be dozens of these environments running with developers working on them.

As decent a plan as this sounds, big corporations usually have an added burden: cost centers. Unfortunately, BubbleCorp can't simply allow developers to log into the AWS Console—where we can manage AWS resources—and spin up environments at will. They needed a way to, among other things, add cost center metadata to the environment to handle their internal billing process.

This brings us to the application we will be focusing on for the remainder of this chapter.

AWS resources dashboard

My team and I were tasked with building a web-based dashboard for AWS. This dashboard would allow developers to log in using their BubbleCorp's credentials and, once authenticated, create new CloudFormation environments as well as visualize the status of each individual resource within a CloudFormation stack.

The application itself is fairly involved, so we will focus on a subset of it: interfacing with the necessary AWS services in order to gather information about the status of each individual resource in a given CloudFormation stack.

Once finished, this is what our simplified dashboard will look like:

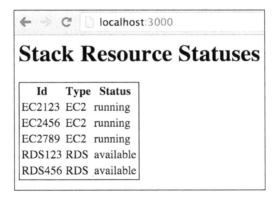

It will display the ID, type, and current status of each resource. This might not seem like much for now, but given that all this information is coming from different, independent web services, it is far too easy to end up with unnecessarily complex code.

We will be using ClojureScript for this and therefore the JavaScript version of the AWS SDK, whose documentation can be found at `http://aws.amazon.com/sdk-for-node-js/`.

Before we get started, let's have a look at each of the AWS Services APIs we will be interacting with.

> In reality, we will not be interacting with the real AWS services but rather a stub server provided for download from the book's GitHub repository.
>
> The reason for this is to make following this chapter easier, as you won't need to create an account as well as generate an API access key to interact with AWS.
>
> Additionally, creating resources incurs cost, and the last thing I want is for you to be charged hundreds of dollars at the end of the month because someone accidentally left resources running for longer than they should—trust me it has happened before.

CloudFormation

The first service we will look at is CloudFormation. This makes sense as the APIs found in here will give us a starting point for finding information about the resources in a given stack.

The describeStacks endpoint

This endpoint is responsible for listing all stacks associated with a particular AWS account. For a given stack, its response looks like the following:

```
{"Stacks"
  [{"StackId"
    "arn:aws:cloudformation:ap-southeast-2:337944750480:stack/
DevStack-62031/1",
    "StackStatus" "CREATE_IN_PROGRESS",
    "StackName" "DevStack-62031",
    "Parameters" [{"ParameterKey" "DevDB", "ParameterValue" nil}]}]}
```

Unfortunately, it doesn't say anything about which resources belong to this stack. It does, however, give us the stack name, which we can use to look up resources in the next service.

The describeStackResources endpoint

This endpoint receives many arguments, but the one we're interested in is the stack name, which, once provided, returns the following:

```
{"StackResources"
  [{"PhysicalResourceId" "EC2123",
    "ResourceType" "AWS::EC2::Instance"},
   {"PhysicalResourceId" "EC2456",
    "ResourceType" "AWS::EC2::Instance"}
   {"PhysicalResourceId" "EC2789",
    "ResourceType" "AWS::EC2::Instance"}
   {"PhysicalResourceId" "RDS123",
    "ResourceType" "AWS::RDS::DBInstance"}
   {"PhysicalResourceId" "RDS456",
    "ResourceType" "AWS::RDS::DBInstance"}]}
```

We seem to be getting somewhere now. This stack has several resources: three EC2 instances and two RDS instances—not too bad for only two API calls.

However, as we mentioned previously, our dashboard needs to show the status of each of the resources. With the list of resource IDs at hand, we need to look to other services that could give us detailed information about each resource.

EC2

The next service we will look at is specific to EC2. As we will see, the responses of the different services aren't as consistent as we would like them to be.

The describeInstances endpoint

This endpoint sounds promising. Based on the documentation, it seems we can give it a list of instance IDs and it will give us back the following response:

```
{"Reservations"
  [{"Instances"
    [{"InstanceId" "EC2123",
      "Tags"
      [{"Key" "StackType", "Value" "Dev"}
       {"Key" "junkTag", "Value" "should not be included"}
       {"Key" "aws:cloudformation:logical-id", "Value" "theDude"}],
      "State" {"Name" "running"}}
     {"InstanceId" "EC2456",
```

```
       "Tags"
       [{"Key" "StackType", "Value" "Dev"}
        {"Key" "junkTag", "Value" "should not be included"}
        {"Key" "aws:cloudformation:logical-id", "Value" "theDude"}],
       "State" {"Name" "running"}}
     {"InstanceId" "EC2789",
      "Tags"
      [{"Key" "StackType", "Value" "Dev"}
       {"Key" "junkTag", "Value" "should not be included"}
       {"Key" "aws:cloudformation:logical-id", "Value" "theDude"}],
       "State" {"Name" "running"}}]}]}
```

Buried in this response, we can see the `State` key, which gives us the status of that particular EC2 instance. This is all we need as far as EC2 goes. This leaves us with RDS to handle.

RDS

One might be tempted to think that getting the statuses of RDS instances would be just as easy as with EC2. Let's see if that is the case.

The describeDBInstances endpoint

This endpoint is equivalent in purpose to the analogous EC2 endpoint we just looked at. Its input, however, is slightly different: it accepts a single instance ID as input and, as of the time of this writing, doesn't support filters.

This means that if our stack has multiple RDS instances—say, in a primary/replica setup—we need to make multiple API calls to gather information about each one of them. Not a big deal, of course, but a limitation to be aware of.

Once given a specific database instance ID, this service responds with the following code:

```
{"DBInstances"
   [{"DBInstanceIdentifier" "RDS123", "DBInstanceStatus"
"available"}]}
```

The fact that a single instance comes inside a vector hints at the fact that filtering will be supported in the future. It just hasn't happened yet.

Designing the solution

We now have all the information we need to start designing our application. We need to coordinate four different API calls per CloudFormation stack:

- `describeStacks`: To list all available stacks
- `describeStackResources`: To retrieve details of all resources contained in a stack
- `describeInstances`: To retrieve details of all EC2 instances in a stack
- `describeDBInstances`: To retrieve details of all DB2 instances in a stack

Next, I would like you to step back for a moment and think about how you would design code like this. Go ahead, I'll wait.

Now that you're back, let's have a look at one possible approach.

If we recall the screenshot of what the dashboard would look like, we realize that, for the purposes of our application, the difference between EC2 and RDS resources can be completely ignored so long as each one has the attributes ID, type, and status.

This means whatever our solution may be, it has to somehow provide a uniform way of abstracting the different resource types.

Additionally, apart from `describeStacks` and `describeStackResources`, which need to be called sequentially, `describeInstances` and `describeDBInstances` can be executed concurrently, after which we will need a way to merge the results.

Since an image is worth a thousand words, the following image is what we would like the workflow to look like:

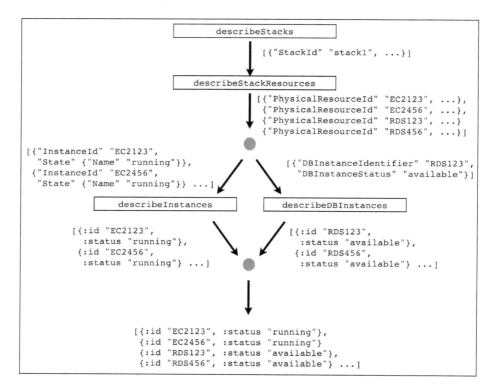

The preceding image highlights a number of key aspects of our solution:

- We start by retrieving stacks by calling `describeStacks`

- Next, for each stack, we call `describeStackResources` to retrieve a list of resources for each one

- Then, we split the list by type, ending with a list of EC2 and one with RDS resources

- We proceed by concurrently calling `describeInstances` and `describeDBInstances`, yielding two lists of results, one per resource type

- As the response formats are different, we transform each resource into a uniform representation

- Lastly, we merge all results into a single list, ready for rendering

This is quite a bit to take in, but as you will soon realize, our solution isn't too far off this high-level description.

We can quite easily think of this problem as having information about several different types of instances flowing through this graph of API calls—being transformed as needed in between—until we arrive at the information we're after, in the format we would like to work with.

As it turns out, a great way to model this problem is to use one of the Reactive abstractions we learned about earlier in this book: Observables.

Running the AWS stub server

Before we jump into writing our dashboard, we should make sure our AWS stub server is properly set up. The stub server is a Clojure web application that simulates how the real AWS API behaves and is the backend our dashboard will talk to.

Let's start by going into our terminal, cloning the book repository using Git and then starting the stub server:

```
$ git clone https://github.com/leonardoborges/ClojureReactiveProgramming
$ cd ClojureReactiveProgramming/code/chapter09/aws-api-stub
$ lein ring server-headless 3001
2014-11-23 17:33:37.766:INFO:oejs.Server:jetty-7.6.8.v20121106
2014-11-23 17:33:37.812:INFO:oejs.AbstractConnector:Started
SelectChannelConnector@0.0.0.0:3001
Started server on port 3001
```

This will have started the server on port 3001. To validate it is working as expected, point your browser to `http://localhost:3001/cloudFormation/describeStacks`. You should see the following JSON response:

```
{
    "Stacks": [
        {
            "Parameters": [
                {
                    "ParameterKey": "DevDB",
                    "ParameterValue": null
                }
            ],
            "StackStatus": "CREATE_IN_PROGRESS",
            "StackId": "arn:aws:cloudformation:ap-southeast-
2:337944750480:stack/DevStack-62031/1",
            "StackName": "DevStack-62031"
        }
    ]
}
```

Setting up the dashboard project

As we previously mentioned, we will be developing the dashboard using ClojureScript with the UI rendered using Om. Additionally, as we have chosen Observables as our main Reactive abstraction, we will need RxJS, one of the many implementations of Microsoft's Reactive Extensions. We will be pulling these dependencies into our project shortly.

Let's create a new ClojureScript project called `aws-dash` using the `om-start` leiningen template:

```
$ lein new om-start aws-dash
```

This gives us a starting point, but we should make sure our versions all match. Open up the `project.clj` file found in the root directory of the new project and ensure the dependencies section looks like the following:

```
. . .
    :dependencies [[org.clojure/clojure "1.6.0"]
                   [org.clojure/clojurescript "0.0-2371"]
                   [org.clojure/core.async "0.1.346.0-17112a-alpha"]
                   [om "0.5.0"]
                   [com.facebook/react "0.9.0"]
                   [cljs-http "0.1.20"]
                   [com.cognitect/transit-cljs "0.8.192"]]
    :plugins [[lein-cljsbuild "1.0.3"]]
. . .
```

This is the first time we see the last two dependencies. `cljs-http` is a simple HTTP library we will use to make AJAX requests to our AWS stub server. `transit-cljs` allows us to, among other things, parse JSON responses into ClojureScript data structures.

 Transit itself is a format and a set of libraries through which applications developed in different technologies can speak to each other. In this case, we are using the Clojurescript library to parse JSON, but if you're interested in learning more, I recommend reading the official blog post announcement by Rich Hickey at `http://blog.cognitect.com/blog/2014/7/22/transit`.

Next, we need RxJS, which, being a JavaScript dependency, isn't available via leiningen. That's OK. We will simply download it into the application output directory, `aws-dash/dev-resources/public/js/`:

```
$ cd aws-dash/dev-resources/public/js/
$ wget https://raw.githubusercontent.com/Reactive-Extensions/RxJS/master/
dist/rx.all.js
--2014-11-23 18:00:21--  https://raw.githubusercontent.com/Reactive-
Extensions/RxJS/master/dist/rx.all.js
Resolving raw.githubusercontent.com... 103.245.222.133
Connecting to raw.githubusercontent.com|103.245.222.133|:443...
connected.
HTTP request sent, awaiting response... 200 OK
Length: 355622 (347K) [text/plain]
Saving to: 'rx.all.js'

100%[========================>] 355,622       966KB/s   in 0.4s

2014-11-23 18:00:24 (966 KB/s) - 'rx.all.js' saved [355622/355622]
```

Moving on, we need to make our application aware of our new dependency on RxJS. Open the `aws-dash/dev-resources/public/index.html` file and add a script tag to pull in RxJS:

```html
<html>
  <body>
    <div id="app"></div>
    <script src="http://fb.me/react-0.9.0.js"></script>
    <script src="js/rx.all.js"></script>
    <script src="js/aws_dash.js"></script>
  </body>
</html>
```

With all the dependencies in place, let's start the auto-compilation for our ClojureScript source files as follows:

```
$ cd aws-dash/
$ lein cljsbuild auto
Compiling ClojureScript.
Compiling "dev-resources/public/js/aws_dash.js" from ("src/cljs" "dev-
resources/tools/repl")...
Successfully compiled "dev-resources/public/js/aws_dash.js" in 0.981
seconds.
```

Creating AWS Observables

We're now ready to start implementing our solution. If you recall from the Reactive Extensions chapter, `RxJava/RxJS/RxClojure` ship with several useful Observables. However, when the built-in Observables aren't enough, it gives us the tools to build our own.

Since it is highly unlikely RxJS already provides Observables for Amazon's AWS API, we will start by implementing our own primitive Observables.

To keep things neat, we will do this in a new file, under `aws-dash/src/cljs/aws_ dash/observables.cljs`:

```
(ns aws-dash.observables
  (:require-macros [cljs.core.async.macros :refer [go]])
  (:require [cljs-http.client :as http]
            [cljs.core.async :refer [<!]]
            [cognitect.transit :as t]))



(def r (t/reader :json))

(def  aws-endpoint "http://localhost:3001")
(defn aws-uri [path]
  (str aws-endpoint path))
```

The namespace declaration requires the necessary dependencies we will need in this file. Note how there is no explicit dependency on RxJS. Since it is a JavaScript dependency that we manually pulled in, it is globally available for us to use via JavaScript interoperability.

The next line sets up a `transit` reader for JSON, which we will use when parsing the stub server responses.

Then, we define the endpoint we will be talking to as well as a helper function to build the correct URIs. Make sure the variable `aws-endpoint` matches the host and port of the stub server started in the previous section.

All Observables we are about to create follow a common structure: they make a request to the stub server, extract some information from the response, optionally transforming it, and then emit each item in the transformed sequence into the new Observable sequence.

To avoid repetition, this pattern is captured in the following function:

```
(defn observable-seq [uri transform]
  (.create js/Rx.Observable
          (fn [observer]
             (go (let [response      (<! (http/get uri {:with-
credentials? false}))
                        data          (t/read r (:body response))
                        transformed   (transform data)]
                   (doseq [x transformed]
                     (.onNext observer x))
                   (.onCompleted observer)))
           (fn [] (.log js/console "Disposed"))))))
```

Let's break this function down:

- observable-seq receives two arguments: the backend URI to which we will issue a GET request, and a transform function which is given the raw parsed JSON response and returns a sequence of transformed items.

- Then, it calls the create function of the RxJS object Rx.Observable. Note how we make use of JavaScript interoperability here: we access the create function by prepending it with a dot much like in Java interoperability. Since Rx.Observable is a global object, we access it by prepending the global JavaScript namespace ClojureScript makes available to our program, js/Rx.Observable.

- The Observable's create function receives two arguments. One is a function that gets called with an Observer to which we can push items to be published in the Observable sequence. The second function is a function that is called whenever this Observable is disposed of. This is the function where we could perform any cleanup needed. In our case, this function simply logs the fact that it is called to the console.

The first function is the one that interests us though:

```
(fn [observer]
  (go (let [response      (<! (http/get uri
                                       {:with-credentials?
                                        false}))
             data          (t/read r (:body response))
             transformed   (transform data)]
        (doseq [x transformed]
          (.onNext observer x))
        (.onCompleted observer))))
```

As soon as it gets called, it performs a request to the provided URI using cljs-http's `get` function, which returns a `core.async` channel. That's why the whole logic is inside a `go` block.

Next, we use the transit JSON reader we configured previously to parse the body of the response, feeding the result into the `transform` function. Remember this function, as per our design, returns a sequence of things. Therefore, all that is left to do is push each item into the observer in turn.

Once we're done, we indicate that this Observable sequence won't emit any new item by invoking the `.onCompleted` function of the `observer` object.

Now, we can proceed creating our Observables using this helper function, starting with the one responsible for retrieving CloudFormation stacks:

```
(defn describe-stacks []
  (observable-seq (aws-uri "/cloudFormation/describeStacks")
                  (fn [data]
                    (map (fn [stack] {:stack-id   (stack "StackId")
                                      :stack-name (stack "StackName")})
                      (data "Stacks")))))
```

This creates an observable that will emit one item per stack, in the following format:

```
({:stack-id "arn:aws:cloudformation:ap-southeast-2:337944750480:stack/
DevStack-62031/1", :stack-name "DevStack-62031"})
```

Now that we have stacks, we need an Observable to describe its resources:

```
(defn describe-stack-resources [stack-name]
  (observable-seq (aws-uri "/cloudFormation/describeStackResources")
                  (fn [data]
                    (map (fn [resource]
                           {:resource-id (resource
"PhysicalResourceId")
                            :resource-type (resource "ResourceType")}
)
                      (data "StackResources")))))
```

It has a similar purpose and emits resource items in the following format:

```
({:resource-id "EC2123", :resource-type "AWS::EC2::Instance"}
 {:resource-id "EC2456", :resource-type "AWS::EC2::Instance"}
 {:resource-id "EC2789", :resource-type "AWS::EC2::Instance"}
 {:resource-id "RDS123", :resource-type "AWS::RDS::DBInstance"}
 {:resource-id "RDS456", :resource-type "AWS::RDS::DBInstance"})
```

Since we're following our strategy almost to the letter, we need two more observables, one for each instance type:

```
(defn describe-instances [instance-ids]
  (observable-seq (aws-uri "/ec2/describeInstances")
                  (fn [data]
                     (let [instances (mapcat (fn [reservation]
                                                (reservation
"Instances"))
                                             (data "Reservations"))]
                        (map (fn [instance]
                               {:instance-id  (instance "InstanceId")
                                :type         "EC2"
                                :status       (get-in instance ["State"
"Name"])})
                             instances)))))

(defn describe-db-instances [instance-id]
  (observable-seq (aws-uri (str "/rds/describeDBInstances/" instance-
id))
                  (fn [data]
                     (map (fn [instance]
                            {:instance-id (instance
"DBInstanceIdentifier")
                             :type          "RDS"
                             :status        (instance
"DBInstanceStatus")})
                          (data "DBInstances")))))
```

Each of which will emit resource items in the following formats for EC2 and RDS, respectively:

```
({:instance-id "EC2123", :type "EC2", :status "running"} ...)
({:instance-id "RDS123", :type "RDS", :status "available"} ...)
```

Combining the AWS Observables

It seems we have all major pieces in place now. All that is left to do is to combine the more primitive, basic Observables we just created into more complex and useful ones by combining them to aggregate all the data we need in order to render our dashboard.

We will start by creating a function that combines both the describe-stacks and describe-stack-resources Observables:

```
(defn stack-resources []
  (-> (describe-stacks)
      (.map #(:stack-name %))
      (.flatMap describe-stack-resources)))
```

Starting in the previous example, we begin to see how defining our API calls in terms of Observable sequences pays off: it's almost simple combining these two Observables in a declarative manner.

Remember the role of `flatMap`: as `describe-stack-resources` itself returns an Observable, we use `flatMap` to flatten both Observables, as we have done before in various different abstractions.

The `stack-resources` Observable will emit resource items for all stacks. According to our plan, we would like to fork the processing here in order to concurrently retrieve EC2 and RDS instance data.

By following this train of thought, we arrive at two more functions that combine and transform the previous Observables:

```
(defn ec2-instance-status [resources]
  (-> resources
      (.filter #(= (:resource-type %) "AWS::EC2::Instance"))
      (.map #(:resource-id %))
      (.reduce conj [])
      (.flatMap describe-instances)))

(defn rds-instance-status [resources]
  (-> resources
      (.filter #(= (:resource-type %) "AWS::RDS::DBInstance"))
      (.map #(:resource-id %))
      (.flatMap describe-db-instances)))
```

Both the functions receive an argument, resources, which is the result of calling the `stack-resources` Observable. That way, we only need to call it once.

Once again, it is fairly simple to combine the Observables in a way that makes sense, following our high-level idea described previously.

Starting with `resources`, we filter out the types we're not interested in, retrieve its IDs, and request its detailed information by flatmapping the `describe-instances` and `describe-db-instances` Observables.

Note, however, that due to a limitation in the RDS API described earlier, we have to call it multiple times to retrieve information about all RDS instances.

This seemingly fundamental difference in how we use the API becomes a minor transformation in our EC2 observable, which simply accumulates all IDs into a vector so that we can retrieve them all at once.

Our simple Reactive API to Amazon AWS is now complete, leaving us with the UI to create.

Putting it all together

Let's now turn to building our user interface. It's a simple one, so let's just jump into it. Open up `aws-dash/src/cljs/aws_dash/core.cljs` and add the following:

```clojure
(ns aws-dash.core
  (:require [aws-dash.observables :as obs]
            [om.core :as om :include-macros true]
            [om.dom :as dom :include-macros true]))

(enable-console-print!)

(def app-state (atom {:instances []}))

(defn instance-view [{:keys [instance-id type status]} owner]
  (reify
    om/IRender
    (render [this]
      (dom/tr nil
              (dom/td nil instance-id)
              (dom/td nil type)
              (dom/td nil status)))))

(defn instances-view [instances owner]
  (reify
    om/IRender
    (render [this]
      (apply dom/table #js {:style #js {:border "1px solid black;"}}
             (dom/tr nil
                     (dom/th nil "Id")
                     (dom/th nil "Type")
                     (dom/th nil "Status"))
             (om/build-all instance-view instances)))))

(om/root
 (fn [app owner]
   (dom/div nil
            (dom/h1 nil "Stack Resource Statuses")
            (om/build instances-view (:instances app))))
 app-state
 {:target (. js/document (getElementById "app"))})
```

Our application state contains a single key, `:instances`, which starts as an empty vector. As we can see from each Om component, instances will be rendered as rows in a HTML table.

After saving the file, make sure the web server is running by starting it from the REPL:

```
lein repl
Compiling ClojureScript.
nREPL server started on port 58209 on host 127.0.0.1 -
nrepl://127.0.0.1:58209
REPL-y 0.3.5, nREPL 0.2.6
Clojure 1.6.0
Java HotSpot(TM) 64-Bit Server VM 1.8.0_25-b17
    Docs: (doc function-name-here)
          (find-doc "part-of-name-here")
  Source: (source function-name-here)
 Javadoc: (javadoc java-object-or-class-here)
    Exit: Control+D or (exit) or (quit)
 Results: Stored in vars *1, *2, *3, an exception in *e


user=> (run)
2015-02-08 21:02:34.503:INFO:oejs.Server:jetty-7.6.8.v20121106
2015-02-08 21:02:34.545:INFO:oejs.AbstractConnector:Started
SelectChannelConnector@0.0.0.0:3000
#<Server org.eclipse.jetty.server.Server@35bc3669>
```

You should now be able point your browser to http://localhost:3000/, but, as you might have guessed, you will see nothing but an empty table.

This is because we haven't yet used our Reactive AWS API.

Let's fix it and bring it all together at the bottom of core.cljs:

```
(def resources (obs/stack-resources))

(.subscribe (-> (.merge  (obs/rds-instance-status resources)
                         (obs/ec2-instance-status resources))
                (.reduce conj []))
            #(swap! app-state assoc :instances %))
```

Yes, this is all we need! We create a stack-resources Observable and pass it as an argument to both rds-instance-status and ec2-instance-status, which will concurrently retrieve status information about all instances.

Next, we create a new Observable by merging the previous two followed by a call to .reduce, which will accumulate all information into a vector, convenient for rendering.

Finally, we simply subscribe to this Observable and, when it emits its results, we simply update our application state, leaving Om to do all the rendering for us.

Save the file and make sure ClojureScript has compiled successfully. Then, go back to your browser at `http://localhost:3000/`, and you should see all instance statuses, as pictured at the beginning of this chapter.

Exercises

With our previous approach, the only way to see new information about the AWS resources is by refreshing the whole page. Modify our implementation in such a way that it queries the stub services every so often—say, every 500 milliseconds.

 The `interval` function from RxJS can be helpful in solving this exercise. Think how you might use it together with our existing stream by reviewing how `flatMap` works.

Summary

In this chapter, we looked at a real use case for Reactive applications: building a dashboard for AWS CloudFormation stacks.

We have seen how thinking of all the information needed as resources/items flowing through a graph fits nicely with how one creates Observables.

In addition, by creating primitive Observables that do one thing only gives us a nice declarative way to combine them into more complex Observables, giving us a degree of reuse not usually found with common techniques.

Finally, we packaged it together with a simple Om-based interface to demonstrate how using different abstractions in the same application does not add to complexity as long as the abstractions are chosen carefully for the problem at hand.

This brings us to the end of what hopefully was an enjoyable and informative journey through the different ways of Reactive Programming.

Far from being a complete reference, this book aims to provide you, the reader, with enough information, as well as concrete tools and examples that you can apply today.

It is also my hope that the references and exercises included in this book prove themselves useful, should you wish to expand your knowledge and seek out more details.

Lastly, I strongly encourage you to turn the page and read the *Appendix, The Algebra of Library Design,* as I truly believe it will, if nothing else, make you think hard about the importance of composition in programming.

I sincerely wish this book has been as entertaining and instructional to read as it was to write.

Thank you for reading. I look forward to seeing the great things you build.

The Algebra of Library Design

You might have noticed that all reactive abstractions we have encountered in this book have a few things in common. For one, they work as "container-like" abstractions:

- Futures encapsulate a computation that eventually yields a single value
- Observables encapsulate computations that can yield multiple values over time in the shape of a stream
- Channels encapsulate values pushed to them and can have them popped from it, working as a concurrent queue through which concurrent processes communicate

Then, once we have this "container," we can operate on it in a number of ways, which are very similar across the different abstractions and frameworks: we can `filter` the values contained in them, transform them using `map`, combine abstractions of the same type using `bind`/`flatMap`/`selectMany`, execute multiple computations in parallel, aggregate the results using `sequence`, and much more.

As such, even though the abstractions and their underlying workings are fundamentally different, it still feels they belong to some type of higher-level abstractions.

In this appendix, we will explore what these higher-level abstractions are, the relationship between them, and how we can take advantage of them in our projects.

The semantics of map

We will get started by taking a look at one of the most used operations in these abstractions: map.

We've been using map for a long time in order to transform sequences. Thus, instead of creating a new function name for each new abstraction, library designers simply abstract the map operation over its own container type.

Imagine the mess we would end up in if we had functions such as transform-observable, transform-channel, combine-futures, and so on.

Thankfully, this is not the case. The semantics of map are well understood to the point that even if a developer hasn't used a specific library before, he will almost always assume that map will apply a function to the value(s) contained within whatever abstraction the library provides.

Let's look at three examples we encountered in this book. We will create a new leiningen project in which to experiment with the contents of this appendix:

```
$ lein new library-design
```

Next, let's add a few dependencies to our project.clj file:

```
    . . .
    :dependencies [[org.clojure/clojure "1.6.0"]
                   [com.leonardoborges/imminent "0.1.0"]
                   [com.netflix.rxjava/rxjava-clojure "0.20.7"]
                   [org.clojure/core.async "0.1.346.0-17112a-alpha"]
                   [uncomplicate/fluokitten "0.3.0"]]
    . . .
```

Don't worry about the last dependency — we'll get to it later on.

Now, start an REPL session so that we can follow along:

```
$ lein repl
```

Then, enter the following into your REPL:

```
(require '[imminent.core :as i]
         '[rx.lang.clojure.core :as rx]
         '[clojure.core.async :as async])

(def  repl-out *out*)
(defn prn-to-repl [& args]
  (binding [*out* repl-out]
    (apply prn args)))
```

```
(-> (i/const-future 31)
    (i/map #(* % 2))
    (i/on-success #(prn-to-repl (str "Value: " %))))


(as-> (rx/return 31) obs
    (rx/map #(* % 2) obs)
    (rx/subscribe obs #(prn-to-repl (str "Value: " %))))

(def c        (chan))
(def mapped-c (async/map< #(* % 2) c))

(async/go (async/>! c 31))
(async/go (prn-to-repl (str "Value: " (async/<! mapped-c))))

"Value: 62"
"Value: 62"
"Value: 62"
```

The three examples — using imminent, RxClojure, and core.async, respectively — look remarkably similar. They all follow a simple recipe:

1. Put the number 31 inside their respective abstraction.
2. Double that number by mapping a function over the abstraction.
3. Print its result to the REPL.

As expected, this outputs the value 62 three times to the screen.

It would seem map performs the same abstract steps in all three cases: it applies the provided function, puts the resulting value in a fresh new container, and returns it. We could continue generalizing, but we would just be rediscovering an abstraction that already exists: Functors.

Functors

Functors are the first abstraction we will look at and they are rather simple: they define a single operation called fmap. In Clojure, Functors can be represented using protocols and are used for containers that can be mapped over. Such containers include, but are not limited to, lists, Futures, Observables, and channels.

The *Algebra* in the title of this *Appendix* refers to **Abstract Algebra**, a branch of Mathematics that studies algebraic structures. An algebraic structure is, to put it simply, a set with one or more operations defined on it.

As an example, consider **Semigroups**, which is one such algebraic structure. It is defined to be a set of elements together with an operation that combines any two elements of this set. Therefore, the set of positive integers together with the addition operation form a Semigroup.

Another tool used for studying algebraic structures is called Category Theory, of which Functors are part of.

We won't delve too much into the theory behind all this, as there are plenty of books [9][10] available on the subject. It was, however, a necessary detour to explain the title used in this appendix.

Does this mean all of these abstractions implement a Functor protocol? Unfortunately, this is not the case. As Clojure is a dynamic language and it didn't have protocols built in — they were added in version 1.2 of the language — these frameworks tend to implement their own version of the map function, which doesn't belong to any protocol in particular.

The only exception is imminent, which implements the protocols included in fluokitten, a Clojure library providing concepts from Category theory such as Functors.

This is a simplified version of the Functor protocol found in fluokitten:

```
(defprotocol Functor
  (fmap [fv g]))
```

As mentioned previously, Functors define a single operation. fmap applies the function g to whatever value is inside the container, Functor, fv.

However, implementing this protocol does not guarantee that we have actually implemented a Functor. This is because, in addition to implementing the protocol, Functors are also required to obey a couple of laws, which we will examine briefly.

The identity law is as follows:

```
(= (fmap a-functor identity)
   (identity a-functor))
```

The preceding code is all we need to verify this law. It simply says that mapping the `identity` function over `a-functor` is the same as simply applying the `identity` function to the Functor itself.

The composition law is as follows:

```
(= (fmap a-functor (comp f g))
   (fmap (fmap a-functor g) f))
```

The composition law, in turn, says that if we compose two arbitrary functions `f` and `g`, take the resulting function and apply that to `a-functor`, that is the same as mapping `g` over the Functor and then mapping `f` over the resulting Functor.

No amount of text will be able to replace practical examples, so we will implement our own Functor, which we will call `Option`. We will then revisit the laws to ensure we have respected them.

The Option Functor

As Tony Hoare once put it, null references are his one billion dollar mistake (http://www.infoq.com/presentations/Null-References-The-Billion-Dollar-Mistake-Tony-Hoare). Regardless of background, you no doubt will have encountered versions of the dreadful `NullPointerException`. This usually happens when we try to call a method on an object reference that is `null`.

Clojure embraces null values due to its interoperability with Java, its host language, but it provides improved support for dealing with them.

The core library is packed with functions that do the right thing if passed a nil value—Clojure's version of Java's `null`. For instance, how many elements are there in a `nil` sequence?

```
(count nil) ;; 0
```

Thanks to conscious design decisions regarding `nil`, we can, for the most part, afford not worry about it. For all other cases, the `Option` Functor might be of some help.

The remaining of the examples in this appendix should be in a file called `option.clj` under `library-design/src/library_design/`. You're welcome to try this in the REPL as well.

Let's start our next example by adding the namespace declaration as well as the data we will be working with:

```
(ns library-design.option
  (:require [uncomplicate.fluokitten.protocols :as fkp]
```

```
                    [uncomplicate.fluokitten.core :as fkc]
                    [uncomplicate.fluokitten.jvm :as fkj]
                    [imminent.core :as I]))

(def pirates [{:name "Jack Sparrow"     :born 1700 :died 1740 :ship
"Black Pearl"}
              {:name "Blackbeard"       :born 1680 :died 1750 :ship
"Queen Anne's Revenge"}
              {:name "Hector Barbossa" :born 1680 :died 1740 :ship
nil}])

(defn pirate-by-name [name]
  (->> pirates
       (filter #(= name (:name %)))
       first))

(defn age [{:keys [born died]}]
  (- died born))
```

As a Pirates of the Caribbean fan, I thought it would be interesting to play with pirates for this example. Let's say we would like to calculate Jack Sparrow's age. Given the data and functions we just covered, this is a simple task:

```
(-> (pirate-by-name "Jack Sparrow")
    age) ;; 40
```

However, what if we would like to know Davy Jones' age? We don't actually have any data for this pirate, so if we run our program again, this is what we'll get:

```
(-> (pirate-by-name "Davy Jones")
    age) ;; NullPointerException    clojure.lang.Numbers.ops
(Numbers.java:961)
```

There it is. The dreadful `NullPointerException`. This happens because in the implementation of the age function, we end up trying to subtract two `nil` values, which is incorrect. As you might have guessed, we will attempt to fix this by using the `Option` Functor.

Traditionally, `Option` is implemented as an algebraic data type, more specifically a sum type with two variants: `Some` and `None`. These variants are used to identify whether a value is present or not without using `nil`s. You can think of both `Some` and `None` as subtypes of `Option`.

In Clojure, we will represent them using records:

```
(defrecord Some [v])

(defrecord None [])

(defn option [v]
  (if v
    (Some. v)
    (None.)))
```

As we can see, Some can contain a single value whereas None contains nothing. It's simply a marker indicating the absence of content. We have also created a helper function called option, which creates the appropriate record depending on whether its argument is nil or not.

The next step is to extend the Functor protocol to both records:

```
(extend-protocol fkp/Functor
  Some
  (fmap [f g]
    (Some. (g (:v f))))
  None
  (fmap [_ _]
    (None.)))
```

Here's where the semantic meaning of the Option Functor becomes apparent: as Some contains a value, its implementation of fmap simply applies the function g to the value inside the Functor f, which is of type Some. Finally, we put the result inside a new Some record.

Now what does it mean to map a function over a None? You probably guessed that it doesn't really make sense — the None record holds no values. The only thing we can do is return another None. As we will see shortly, this gives the Option Functor a short-circuiting semantic.

In the fmap implementation of None, we could have returned a reference to this instead of a new record instance. I've not done so simply to make it clear that we need to return an instance of None.

Now that we've implemented the Functor protocol, we can try it out:

```
(->> (option (pirate-by-name "Jack Sparrow"))
     (fkc/fmap age)) ;; #library_design.option.Some{:v 40}

(->> (option (pirate-by-name "Davy Jones"))
     (fkc/fmap age)) ;; #library_design.option.None{}
```

The first example shouldn't hold any surprises. We convert the pirate map we get from calling `pirate-by-name` into an option, and then `fmap` the age function over it.

The second example is the interesting one. As stated previously, we have no data about Davy Jones. However, mapping `age` over it does not throw an exception any longer, instead returning `None`.

This might seem like a small benefit, but the bottom line is that the `Option` Functor makes it safe to chain operations together:

```
(->> (option (pirate-by-name "Jack Sparrow"))
     (fkc/fmap age)
     (fkc/fmap inc)
     (fkc/fmap #(* 2 %))) ;; #library_design.option.Some{:v 82}

(->> (option (pirate-by-name "Davy Jones"))
     (fkc/fmap age)
     (fkc/fmap inc)
     (fkc/fmap #(* 2 %))) ;; #library_design.option.None{}
```

At this point, some readers might be thinking about the `some->` macro—introduced in Clojure 1.5—and how it effectively achieves the same result as the `Option` Functor. This intuition is correct as demonstrated as follows:

```
(some-> (pirate-by-name "Davy Jones")
        age
        inc
        (* 2)) ;; nil
```

The `some->` macro threads the result of the first expression through the first form if it is not `nil`. Then, if the result of that expression isn't `nil`, it threads it through the next form and so on. As soon as any of the expressions evaluates to nil, `some->` short-circuits and returns nil immediately.

That being said, Functor is a much more general concept, so as long as we are working with this concept, our code doesn't need to change as we are operating at a higher level of abstraction:

```
(->> (i/future (pirate-by-name "Jack Sparrow"))
     (fkc/fmap age)
     (fkc/fmap inc)
     (fkc/fmap #(* 2 %))) ;; #<Future@30518bfc: #<Success@39bd662c:
82>>
```

In the preceding example, even though we are working with a fundamentally different tool—futures—the code using the result did not have to change. This is only possible because both Options and futures are Functors and implement the same protocol provided by fluokitten. We have gained composability and simplicity as we can use the same API to work with various different abstractions.

Speaking of composability, this property is guaranteed by the second law of Functors. Let's see if our Option Functor respects this and the first—the identity—laws:

```
;; Identity
(= (fkc/fmap identity (option 1))
   (identity (option 1))) ;; true


;; Composition
(= (fkc/fmap (comp identity inc) (option 1))
   (fkc/fmap identity (fkc/fmap inc (option 1)))) ;; true
```

And we're done, our Option Functor is a lawful citizen. The remaining two abstractions also come paired with their own laws. We will not cover the laws in this section, but I encourage the reader to read about them (http://www.leonardoborges. com/writings/2012/11/30/monads-in-small-bites-part-i-functors/).

Finding the average of ages

In this section, we will explore a different use case for the Option Functor. We would like to, given a number of pirates, calculate the average of their ages. This is simple enough to do:

```
(defn avg [& xs]
  (float (/ (apply + xs) (count xs))))

(let [a (some-> (pirate-by-name "Jack Sparrow") age)
      b (some-> (pirate-by-name "Blackbeard") age)
      c (some-> (pirate-by-name "Hector Barbossa") age)]
  (avg a b c)) ;; 56.666668
```

Note how we are using some-> here to protect us from nil values. Now, what happens if there is a pirate for which we have no information?

```
(let [a (some-> (pirate-by-name "Jack Sparrow") age)
      b (some-> (pirate-by-name "Davy Jones") age)
      c (some-> (pirate-by-name "Hector Barbossa") age)]
  (avg a b c)) ;; NullPointerException   clojure.lang.Numbers.ops
(Numbers.java:961)
```

It seems we're back at square one! It's worse now because using some-> doesn't help if we need to use all values at once, as opposed to threading them through a chain of function calls.

Of course, not all is lost. All we need to do is check if all values are present before calculating the average:

```
(let [a (some-> (pirate-by-name "Jack Sparrow") age)
      b (some-> (pirate-by-name "Davy Jones") age)
      c (some-> (pirate-by-name "Hector Barbossa") age)]
  (when (and a b c)
    (avg a b c))) ;; nil
```

While this works perfectly fine, our implementation suddenly had to become aware that any or all of the values a, b, and c could be nil. The next abstraction we will look at, Applicative Functors, fixes this.

Applicative Functors

Like Functors, **Applicative Functors** are a sort of container and defines two operations:

```
(defprotocol Applicative
  (pure [av v])
  (fapply [ag av]))
```

The pure function is a generic way to put a value inside an Applicative Functor. So far, we have been using the option helper function for this purpose. We will be using it a little later.

The fapply function will unwrap the function contained in the Applicative ag and apply it to the value contained in the applicative av.

The purpose of both the functions will become clear with an example, but first, we need to promote our Option Functor into an Applicative Functor:

```
(extend-protocol fkp/Applicative
  Some
```

```
    (pure [_ v]
      (Some. v))

    (fapply [ag av]
      (if-let [v (:v av)]
        (Some. ((:v ag) v))
        (None.)))

  None
  (pure [_ v]
    (Some. v))

  (fapply [ag av]
    (None.)))
```

The implementation of pure is the simplest. All it does is wrap the value v into an instance of Some. Equally simple is the implementation of fapply for None. As there is no value, we simply return None again.

The fapply implementation of Some ensures both arguments have a value for the :v keyword—strictly speaking they both have to be instances of Some. If :v is non-nil, it applies the function contained in ag to v, finally wrapping the result. Otherwise, it returns None.

This should be enough to try our first example using the Applicative Functor API:

```
(fkc/fapply (option inc) (option 2))
;; #library_design.option.Some{:v 3}

(fkc/fapply (option nil) (option 2))
;; #library_design.option.None{}
```

We are now able to work with Functors that contain functions. Additionally, we have also preserved the semantics of what should happen when any of the Functors don't have a value.

We can now revisit the age average example from before:

```
(def age-option (comp (partial fkc/fmap age) option pirate-by-name))

(let [a (age-option "Jack Sparrow")
      b (age-option "Blackbeard")
      c (age-option "Hector Barbossa")]
  (fkc/<*> (option (fkj/curry avg 3))
           a b c))
;; #library_design.option.Some{:v 56.666668}
```

> The `vararg` function `<*>` is defined by fluokitten and performs a left-associative `fapply` on its arguments. Essentially, it is a convenience function that makes `(<*> f g h)` equivalent to `(fapply (fapply f g) h)`.

We start by defining a helper function to avoid repetition. The `age-option` function retrieves the age of a pirate as an option for us.

Next, we curry the `avg` function to 3 arguments and put it into an option. Then, we use the `<*>` function to apply it to the options a, b, and c. We get to the same result, but have the Applicative Functor take care of nil values for us.

> **Function currying**
>
> Currying is the technique of transforming a function of multiple arguments into a higher-order function of a single argument that returns more single-argument functions until all arguments have been supplied.
>
> Roughly speaking, currying makes the following snippets equivalent:
>
> ```
> (def curried-1 (fkj/curry + 2))
> (def curried-2 (fn [a]
>                    (fn [b]
>                      (+ a b))))
>
>
> ((curried-1 10) 20) ;; 30
> ((curried-2 10) 20) ;; 30
> ```

Using Applicative Functors this way is so common that the pattern has been captured as the function `alift`, as shown in the following:

```
(defn alift
  "Lifts a n-ary function `f` into a applicative context"
  [f]
  (fn [& as]
    {:pre  [(seq as)]}
    (let [curried (fkj/curry f (count as))]
      (apply fkc/<*>
             (fkc/fmap curried (first as))
             (rest as)))))
```

The `alift` function is responsible for lifting a function in such a way that it can be used with Applicative Functors without much ceremony. Because of the assumptions we are able to make about Applicative Functors — for instance, that it is also a Functor — we can write generic code that can be re-used across any Applicatives.

With `alift` in place, our age average example turns into the following:

```
(let [a (age-option "Jack Sparrow")
      b (age-option "Blackbeard")
      c (age-option "Hector Barbossa")]
  ((alift avg) a b c))
;; #library_design.option.Some{:v 56.666668}
```

We lift `avg` into an Applicative compatible version, making the code look remarkably like simple function application. And since we are not doing anything interesting with the let bindings, we can simplify it further as follows:

```
((alift avg) (age-option "Jack Sparrow")
             (age-option "Blackbeard")
             (age-option "Hector Barbossa"))
;; #library_design.option.Some{:v 56.666668}


((alift avg) (age-option "Jack Sparrow")
             (age-option "Davy Jones")
             (age-option "Hector Barbossa"))
;; #library_design.option.None{}
```

As with Functors, we can take the code as it is, and simply replace the underlying abstraction, preventing repetition once again:

```
((alift avg) (i/future (some-> (pirate-by-name "Jack Sparrow") age))
             (i/future (some-> (pirate-by-name "Blackbeard") age))
             (i/future (some-> (pirate-by-name "Hector Barbossa")
age)))
;; #<Future@17b1be96: #<Success@16577601: 56.666668>>
```

Gathering stats about ages

Now that we can safely calculate the average age of a number of pirates, it might be interesting to take this further and calculate the median and standard deviation of the pirates' ages, in addition to their average age.

We already have a function to calculate the average, so let's just create the ones to calculate the median and the standard deviation of a list of numbers:

```
(defn median [& ns]
  (let [ns (sort ns)
        cnt (count ns)
        mid (bit-shift-right cnt 1)]
    (if (odd? cnt)
      (nth ns mid)
      (/ (+ (nth ns mid) (nth ns (dec mid))) 2))))

(defn std-dev [& samples]
  (let [n (count samples)
    mean (/ (reduce + samples) n)
    intermediate (map #(Math/pow (- %1 mean) 2) samples)]
    (Math/sqrt
      (/ (reduce + intermediate) n))))
```

With these functions in place, we can write the code that will gather all the stats for us:

```
(let [a       (some-> (pirate-by-name "Jack Sparrow")    age)
      b       (some-> (pirate-by-name "Blackbeard")      age)
      c       (some-> (pirate-by-name "Hector Barbossa") age)
      avg     (avg a b c)
      median  (median a b c)
      std-dev (std-dev a b c)]
  {:avg avg
   :median median
   :std-dev std-dev})

;; {:avg 56.666668,
;;  :median 60,
;;  :std-dev 12.472191289246473}
```

This implementation is fairly straightforward. We first retrieve all ages we're interested in and bind them to the locals a, b, and c. We then reuse the values when calculating the remaining stats. We finally gather all results in a map for easy access.

By now the reader will probably know where we're headed: what if any of those values is `nil`?

```
(let [a       (some-> (pirate-by-name "Jack Sparrow")     age)
      b       (some-> (pirate-by-name "Davy Jones")       age)
      c       (some-> (pirate-by-name "Hector Barbossa") age)
      avg     (avg a b c)
      median  (median a b c)
      std-dev (std-dev a b c)]
  {:avg avg
   :median median
   :std-dev std-dev})
;; NullPointerException   clojure.lang.Numbers.ops (Numbers.
java:961)
```

The second binding, b, returns `nil`, as we don't have any information about Davy Jones. As such, it causes the calculations to fail. Like before, we can change our implementation to protect us from such failures:

```
(let [a       (some-> (pirate-by-name "Jack Sparrow")     age)
      b       (some-> (pirate-by-name "Davy Jones")       age)
      c       (some-> (pirate-by-name "Hector Barbossa") age)
      avg     (when (and a b c) (avg a b c))
      median  (when (and a b c) (median a b c))
      std-dev (when (and a b c) (std-dev a b c))]
  (when (and a b c)
    {:avg avg
     :median median
     :std-dev std-dev}))
;; nil
```

This time it's even worse than when we only had to calculate the average; the code is checking for `nil` values in four extra spots: before calling the three stats functions and just before gathering the stats into the result map.

Can we do better?

Monads

Our last abstraction will solve the very problem we raised in the previous section: how to safely perform intermediate calculations by preserving the semantics of the abstractions we're working with—in this case, options.

It should be no surprise now that fluokitten also provides a protocol for Monads, simplified and shown as follows:

```
(defprotocol Monad
  (bind [mv g]))
```

If you think in terms of a class hierarchy, Monads would be at the bottom of it, inheriting from Applicative Functors, which, in turn, inherit from Functors. That is, if you're working with a Monad, you can assume it is also an Applicative and a Functor.

The `bind` function of monads takes a function `g` as its second argument. This function receives as input the value contained in `mv` and returns another Monad containing its result. This is a crucial part of the contract: `g` has to return a Monad.

The reason why will become clearer after some examples. But first, let's promote our Option abstraction to a Monad—at this point, Option is already an Applicative Functor and a Functor:

```
(extend-protocol fkp/Monad
  Some
  (bind [mv g]
    (g (:v mv)))

  None
  (bind [_ _]
    (None.)))
```

The implementation is fairly simple. In the `None` version, we can't really do anything, so just like we have been doing so far, we return an instance of `None`.

The `Some` implementation extracts the value from the Monad `mv` and applies the function `g` to it. Note how this time we don't need to wrap the result as the function `g` already returns a Monad instance.

Using the Monad API, we could sum the ages of our pirates as follows:

```
(def opt-ctx (None.))

(fkc/bind (age-option "Jack Sparrow")
          (fn [a]
            (fkc/bind (age-option "Blackbeard")
                      (fn [b]
                        (fkc/bind (age-option "Hector Barbossa")
                                  (fn [c]
                                    (fkc/pure opt-ctx
```

```
                                                    (+ a b c)))))))))
;; #library_design.option.Some{:v 170.0}
```

Firstly, we are making use of Applicative's `pure` function in the inner-most function. Remember that role of `pure` is to provide a generic way to put a value into an Applicative Functor. Since Monads are also Applicative, we make use of them here.

However, since Clojure is a dynamically typed language, we need to hint pure with the context—container—type we wish to use. This context is simply an instance of either `Some` or `None`. They both have the same pure implementation.

While we do get the right answer, the preceding example is far from what we would like to write due to its excessive nesting. It is also hard to read.

Thankfully, fluokitten provides a much better way to write monadic code, called the do-notation:

```
(fkc/mdo [a (age-option "Jack Sparrow")
          b (age-option "Blackbeard")
          c (age-option "Hector Barbossa")]
         (fkc/pure opt-ctx  (+ a b c)))
;; #library_design.option.Some{:v 170.0}
```

Suddenly, the same code becomes a lot cleaner and easier to read, without losing any of the semantics of the Option Monad. This is because `mdo` is a macro that expands to the code equivalent of the nested version, as we can verify by expanding the macro as follows:

```
(require '[clojure.walk :as w])

(w/macroexpand-all '(fkc/mdo [a (age-option "Jack Sparrow")
                              b (age-option "Blackbeard")
                              c (age-option "Hector Barbossa")]
                             (option  (+ a b c))))
;; (uncomplicate.fluokitten.core/bind
;;   (age-option "Jack Sparrow")
;;   (fn*
;;    ([a]
;;     (uncomplicate.fluokitten.core/bind
;;      (age-option "Blackbeard")
;;      (fn*
;;       ([b]
;;        (uncomplicate.fluokitten.core/bind
;;         (age-option "Hector Barbossa")
;;         (fn* ([c] (fkc/pure opt-ctx (+ a b c)))))))))))
```

It is important to stop for a moment here and appreciate the power of Clojure — and Lisp in general.

Languages such as Haskell and Scala, which make heavy use of abstractions such as Functors, Applicative, and Monads, also have their own versions of the do-notation. However, this support is baked into the compiler itself.

As an example, when Haskell added do-notation to the language, a new version of the compiler was released, and developers wishing to use the new feature had to upgrade.

In Clojure, on the other hand, this new feature can be shipped as a library due to the power and flexibility of macros. This is exactly what fluokitten has done.

Now, we are ready to go back to our original problem, gathering stats about the pirates' ages.

First, we will define a couple of helper functions that convert the result of our stats functions into the Option Monad:

```
(def avg-opt     (comp option avg))
(def median-opt  (comp option median))
(def std-dev-opt (comp option std-dev))
```

Here, we take advantage of function composition to create monadic versions of existing functions.

Next, we will rewrite our solution using the monadic do-notation we learned earlier:

```
(fkc/mdo [a       (age-option "Jack Sparrow")
          b       (age-option "Blackbeard")
          c       (age-option "Hector Barbossa")
          avg     (avg-opt a b c)
          median  (median-opt a b c)
          std-dev (std-dev-opt a b c)]
         (option {:avg avg
                  :median median
                  :std-dev std-dev}))
;; #library_design.option.Some{:v {:avg 56.666668,
;;                                  :median 60,
;;                                  :std-dev 12.472191289246473}}
```

This time we were able to write the function as we normally would, without having to worry about whether any values in the intermediate computations are empty or not. This semantic that is the very essence of the Option Monad is still preserved, as can be seen in the following:

```
(fkc/mdo [a        (age-option "Jack Sparrow")
          b        (age-option "Blackbeard")
          c        (age-option "Hector Barbossa")
          avg      (avg-opt a b c)
          median   (median-opt a b c)
          std-dev  (std-dev-opt a b c)]
  (fkc/pure opt-ctx {:avg avg
              :median median
              :std-dev std-dev}))
;; #library_design.option.None{}
```

For the sake of completeness, we will use futures to demonstrate how the do-notation works for any Monad:

```
(def avg-fut     (comp i/future-call avg))
(def median-fut  (comp i/future-call median))
(def std-dev-fut (comp i/future-call std-dev))

(fkc/mdo [a        (i/future (some-> (pirate-by-name "Jack Sparrow")
age))
          b        (i/future (some-> (pirate-by-name "Blackbeard")
age))
          c        (i/future (some-> (pirate-by-name "Hector Barbossa")
age))
          avg      (avg-fut a b c)
          median   (median-fut a b c)
          std-dev  (std-dev-fut a b c)]
  (i/const-future {:avg avg
                   :median median
                   :std-dev std-dev}))
;; #<Future@3fd0b0d0: #<Success@1e08486b: {:avg 56.666668,
;;                                          :median 60,
;;                                          :std-dev
12.472191289246473}>>
```

Summary

This appendix has taken us on a brief tour of the world of category theory. We learned three of its abstractions: Functors, Applicative Functors, and Monads. They were the guiding principle behind imminent's API.

To deepen our knowledge and understanding, we implemented our own Option Monad, a common abstraction used to safely handle the absence of values.

We have also seen that using these abstractions allow us to make some assumptions about our code, as seen in functions such as `alift`. There are many other functions we would normally rewrite over and over again for different purposes, but that can be reused if we recognize our code fits into one of the abstractions learned.

Finally, I hope this encourages readers to explore category theory more, as it will undoubtedly change the way you think. And if I can be so bold, I hope this will also change the way you design libraries in the future.

B

Bibliography

[1] Rene Pardo and Remy Landau, *The World's First Electronic Spreadsheet*:
http://www.renepardo.com/articles/spreadsheet.pdf

[2] Conal Elliott and Paul Hudak, *Functional Reactive Animation*:
http://conal.net/papers/icfp97/icfp97.pdf

[3] Evan Czaplicki, *Elm: Concurrent FRP for Functional GUIs*:
http://elm-lang.org/papers/concurrent-frp.pdf

[4] Erik Meijer, *Subject/Observer is Dual to Iterator*:
http://csl.stanford.edu/~christos/pldi2010.fit/meijer.duality.pdf

[5] Henrik Nilsson, Antony Courtney and John Peterson, *Functional Reactive Programming, Continued*: http://haskell.cs.yale.edu/wp-content/uploads/2011/02/workshop-02.pdf

[6] John Hughes, *Generalising Monads to Arrows*:
http://www.cse.chalmers.se/~rjmh/Papers/arrows.pdf

[7] Zhanyong Wan, Walid Taha and Paul Hudak, *Real-Time FRP*:
http://haskell.cs.yale.edu/wp-content/uploads/2011/02/rt-frp.pdf

[8] Walid Taha, Zhanyong Wan, and Paul Hudak, *Event-Driven FRP*:
http://www.cs.yale.edu/homes/zwan/papers/mcu/efrp.pdf

[9] Benjamin C. Pierce, *Basic Category Theory for Computer Scientists*:
http://www.amazon.com/Category-Computer-Scientists-Foundations-Computing-ebook/dp/B00MG7E5WE/ref=sr_1_7?ie=UTF8&qid=1423484917&sr=8-7&keywords=category+theory

[10] Steve Awodey, *Category Theory (Oxford Logic Guides)*: http://www.amazon.com/Category-Theory-Oxford-Logic-Guides/dp/0199237182/ref=sr_1_2?ie=UTF8&qid=1423484917&sr=8-2&keywords=category+theory

[11] Duncan Coutts, Roman Leshchinskiy, and Don Stewart, *Stream Fusion*:
http://code.haskell.org/~dons/papers/icfp088-coutts.pdf

[12] Philip Wadler, *Transforming programs to eliminate trees*:
http://homepages.inf.ed.ac.uk/wadler/papers/deforest/deforest.ps

Index

M

macros
  reference link 105
ManagedBlocker
  reference link 161
map
  about 184, 185
  Functors 185-187
Mimmo Cosenza
  URL 126
minimal CES framework
  about 77, 78
  behaviors, implementing 88, 89
  event streams, implementing 82-87
  project, setting up 78-81
  public API, designing 81, 82
  respondent application, building 92, 93
  tokens, implementing 82
Monads
  about 33, 197
  bind function 198
  example 200, 201
  using 198
monet
  URL 98

N

Netflix 19

O

object-oriented Reactive
        Programming 11-13
Observables
  combining 177, 178
  creating 23-26, 174-177
  custom Observables, creating 26, 27
  manipulating 27, 28
Observable Sequences 18
Observer design pattern
  about 14, 15, 21, 22
  Iterator interface 22, 23
Om
  about 123
  agile board, creating 135, 136

  Contacts application, building 124
Om Project Management 135
om-start template
  URL 126
onError combinator 34, 35
Option Functor
  about 187-191
  use case 191, 192

P

Purely Functional Data Structures
  about 121
  URL 121

R

RDS
  about 164
  describeDBInstances endpoint 168
  used, for building AWS resources
        dashboard 168
React
  reference link 117
ReactiveCocoa
  about 18
  URL 15
Reactive Extensions. *See* **Rx**
Reactive Programming 1
React.js
  about 120
  functional programming 121, 122
Reagi
  about 115
  comparing, with other CES
        frameworks 115
Relational Database Service. *See* **RDS**
respondent application
  building 92, 93
retry combinator 36, 37
Rx
  about 18, 21, 115
  drawbacks 115
  error handling 34
  flatmap 29-32
  Observables, creating 23-26
  Observables, manipulating 27, 28

RxClojure
  URL 23
RxJava
  about 21
  URL 15, 23
RxJS
  about 21
  URL 2

S

sample combinator 38, 39
Scala 200
ScheduledThreadPoolExecutor pool 43
Semigroups 186
signals 16
sine wave animation
  about 1, 2
  coloring 6, 7
  creating 2-4
  enhancing 8
  time, creating 4-6
  updating 7, 8
sliding buffer 71
stock market monitoring application
  application code, implementing 63-66
  building 41-44
  incidental complexity, removing with
      RxClojure 48-50
  observable rolling averages 50-53
  problems, identifying 47
  rewriting, with core.async 62, 63
  rolling averages, displaying 45-47
stub server
  setting up 171

T

Thread Pool 150
tools.namespace
  URL 86
  using 86
transducers
  about 71-73
  reference link 72
  with core.async 73, 75
transit
  about 172
  URL 172
Trello
  URL 135

V

Virtual DOM 122

Thank you for buying
Clojure Reactive Programming

About Packt Publishing

Packt, pronounced 'packed', published its first book, *Mastering phpMyAdmin for Effective MySQL Management*, in April 2004, and subsequently continued to specialize in publishing highly focused books on specific technologies and solutions.

Our books and publications share the experiences of your fellow IT professionals in adapting and customizing today's systems, applications, and frameworks. Our solution-based books give you the knowledge and power to customize the software and technologies you're using to get the job done. Packt books are more specific and less general than the IT books you have seen in the past. Our unique business model allows us to bring you more focused information, giving you more of what you need to know, and less of what you don't.

Packt is a modern yet unique publishing company that focuses on producing quality, cutting-edge books for communities of developers, administrators, and newbies alike. For more information, please visit our website at www.packtpub.com.

About Packt Open Source

In 2010, Packt launched two new brands, Packt Open Source and Packt Enterprise, in order to continue its focus on specialization. This book is part of the Packt Open Source brand, home to books published on software built around open source licenses, and offering information to anybody from advanced developers to budding web designers. The Open Source brand also runs Packt's Open Source Royalty Scheme, by which Packt gives a royalty to each open source project about whose software a book is sold.

Writing for Packt

We welcome all inquiries from people who are interested in authoring. Book proposals should be sent to author@packtpub.com. If your book idea is still at an early stage and you would like to discuss it first before writing a formal book proposal, then please contact us; one of our commissioning editors will get in touch with you.

We're not just looking for published authors; if you have strong technical skills but no writing experience, our experienced editors can help you develop a writing career, or simply get some additional reward for your expertise.

Mastering Clojure Data Analysis

ISBN: 978-1-78328-413-9   Paperback: 340 pages

Leverage the power and flexibility of Clojure through this practical guide to data analysis

1. Explore the concept of data analysis using established scientific methods combined with the powerful Clojure language.

2. Master Naïve Bayesian Classification, Benford's Law, and much more in Clojure.

3. Learn with the help of examples drawn from exciting, real-world data.

Clojure for Machine Learning

ISBN: 978-1-78328-435-1   Paperback: 292 pages

Successfully leverage advanced machine learning techniques using the Clojure ecosystem

1. Covers a lot of machine learning techniques with Clojure programming.

2. Encompasses precise patterns in data to predict future outcomes using various machine learning techniques.

3. Packed with several machine learning libraries available in the Clojure ecosystem.

Please check **www.PacktPub.com** for information on our titles

Clojure Data Analysis Cookbook

ISBN: 978-1-78216-264-3   Paperback: 342 pages

Over 110 recipes to help you dive into the world of practical data analysis using Clojure

1. Get a handle on the torrent of data the modern Internet has created.

2. Recipes for every stage from collection to analysis.

3. A practical approach to analyzing data to help you make informed decisions.

Clojure High Performance Programming

ISBN: 978-1-78216-560-6   Paperback: 152 pages

Understand performance aspects and write high performance code with Clojure

1. See how the hardware and the JVM impact performance.

2. Learn which Java features to use with Clojure, and how.

3. Deep dive into Clojure's concurrency and state primitives.

Please check **www.PacktPub.com** for information on our titles

www.ingramcontent.com/pod-product-compliance
Lightning Source LLC
LaVergne TN
LVHW081340050326
832903LV00024B/1229